Physical Education Technology Playbook

Darla M. Castelli

Leah Holland Fiorentino

Human Kinetics

Library of Congress Cataloging-in-Publication Data

Castelli, Darla M., 1967-
 Physical education technology playbook / Darla M. Castelli, Leah Holland Fiorentino.
  p. cm.
 Includes bibliographical references.
 ISBN-13: 978-0-7360-6055-4 (soft cover)
 ISBN-10: 0-7360-6055-3 (soft cover)
 1. Physical education and training—Data processing. 2. Physical education and training—Computer network resources. 3. Educational technology. 4. Teaching—Aids and devices. 5. Internet in education. I. Fiorentino, Leah. II. Title.
 GV364.C37 2008
 025.040796—dc22

                         2007028099

ISBN-10: 0-7360-6055-3
ISBN-13: 978-0-7360-6055-4

Copyright © 2008 by Darla M. Castelli and Leah Holland Fiorentino

The technology descriptions and instructions were verified by the authors and were current as of November 2007, unless otherwise noted. New technology and program versions may have become available since that date.

Contact the original provider for technical help or questions on technology, programs, or Web sites.

The Web addresses cited in this text were current as of November 2007, unless otherwise noted.

Acquisitions Editor: Scott Wikgren; **Developmental Editor:** Ragen E. Sanner; **Assistant Editor:** Anne Rumery; **Copyeditor:** Patsy Fortney; **Proofreader:** Ray Vallese; **Permission Manager:** Carly Breeding; **Graphic Designer:** Bob Reuther; **Graphic Artist:** Yvonne Griffith; **Cover Designer:** Keith Blomberg; **Photographer (cover):** Neil Bernstein; **Photographer (interior):** Darla M. Castelli; **Photo Office Assistant:** Jason Allen; **Art Manager:** Kelly Hendren; **Associate Art Manager:** Alan L. Wilborn; **Illustrator:** Accurate Art; **Printer:** United Graphics

Printed in the United States of America   10 9 8 7 6 5 4 3 2 1

Human Kinetics
Web site: www.HumanKinetics.com

United States: Human Kinetics
P.O. Box 5076
Champaign, IL 61825-5076
800-747-4457
e-mail: humank@hkusa.com

Canada: Human Kinetics
475 Devonshire Road Unit 100
Windsor, ON N8Y 2L5
800-465-7301 (in Canada only)
e-mail: info@hkcanada.com

Europe: Human Kinetics
107 Bradford Road
Stanningley
Leeds LS28 6AT, United Kingdom
+44 (0) 113 255 5665
e-mail: hk@hkeurope.com

Australia: Human Kinetics
57A Price Avenue
Lower Mitcham, South Australia 5062
08 8372 0999
e-mail: info@hkaustralia.com

New Zealand: Human Kinetics
Division of Sports Distributors NZ Ltd.
P.O. Box 300 226 Albany
North Shore City
Auckland
0064 9 448 1207
e-mail: info@humankinetics.co.nz

Contents

How to Use This Book and Companion Web Site

Given the societal demands of using technology as a teaching and learning tool in the 21st century, this book intends to guide physical education teachers and their students through the integration of experiential learning modules. The term *module* comes from science education, which uses an inquiry-based mechanism of instruction. Modules are a way of organizing content to promote critical thinking, problem solving, and cooperative learning (Brahler, Quitadamo & Johnson, 2002). A module provides a subject-specific forum for self-directed learning and often contains a title, a standard or expectation, instructions, images, and assessment criteria. In this textbook, each module is organized around the outcomes related to one or two national teacher standards. Specifically, a module aligns a standard with a technology such as digital video or the Internet. Additionally, each module contains a probing question, assignment tasks, and assessment criteria. Unlike other textbooks, which focus exclusively on a single educational level, this book incorporates both preservice teacher learning activities for the university classroom and ready-to-use lesson plans and activities for K-12 learners that can be applied during field experiences or by in-service teachers.

The book provides adequate opportunities for teachers (or, in some cases, teacher educators) to become comfortable with and refine their skills and knowledge of common computer-based technologies, including the Internet, software such as Microsoft Office, physical education–specific software, and digital still and video equipment. Once teachers have enhanced their own abilities, they can introduce lesson plans linked to the national physical education content standards (NASPE, 2004) for their K-12 students. Again, we suggest that the K-12 lesson plans and student worksheets be integrated by undergraduate preservice teachers in their early field experiences.

Many chapters begin with a vignette describing a particular technology being integrated into a physical education context. These vignettes provide a snapshot of a situation in which the technology has been effective. We have personally witnessed or participated in situations similar to those in all of the vignettes. The authenticity of these stories should lend credence to our assertion that technology affects student learning.

Each chapter in this book also contains introductory text related to the education theory supporting the proposed integration. Both of us teach technology courses that require students to enhance their technology skills as well as pedagogically promote effectiveness in the educational setting. We believe that it is important for teachers to understand the foundations of learning activities and not simply rush to implement them.

Most chapters conclude with a description of the learning modules and lesson plans available on the companion Web site. The intent of the teacher modules is to help teachers refine and develop their own skill sets, as well as to help new teachers document their personal growth related to specific standards. Teacher educators should select lesson plans that are relevant to their contexts. For example, some modules and lesson plans in this book require the use of Macintosh computers.

Institutions without access to this hardware should select a similar learning module or lesson plan that is Windows-based.

Chapter 2 provides an overview of the educational research related to the effectiveness of technology-rich educational settings. It describes teacher education technology standards and how teacher education programs attempt to aid preservice teachers in meeting these standards. This is followed by a discussion of how teachers can effectively integrate technology behaviors and, more specifically, prepare for the integration of technology. Prior to implementing technology, teachers should ask, *(1)* How will technology improve teacher efficiency? *(2)* How will the integration of technology foster learning in the student? and *(3)* How does the technology accomplish something that previously could not be accomplished? Responses to these questions should lead to the enhancement of student learning. This chapter encourages teachers to use technology not just to motivate apathetic K-12 students, but also to promote physical activity and enhance students' comprehension of key physical education concepts. This chapter introduces the unique obstacles physical education teachers have to overcome to create technology-rich classes.

Chapter 3 focuses on data entry and how to meaningfully organize information to enhance student learning and teacher effectiveness. Data are often entered into computer software so they can be converted into reports. For example, the chapter provides directions and learning modules related to the Fitnessgram/Activitygram software, which requires the input of student data to create individual and group fitness reports. Before teachers can use software to foster student learning, they must understand basic data entry concepts such as format control and database organization. This chapter helps teachers make decisions regarding the management of information.

The use of spreadsheets and Microsoft Excel software is described in chapter 4. The reader is provided with basic strategies on how to manage student data such as motor performance criteria as well as how to display these data for advocacy purposes. The chapter includes a discussion of the design and development of various charts and graphs. Charts and graphs can be effective means of communicating data, but only if their complexity matches the needs of the audience.

In chapter 5 teachers are asked to become safe, knowledgeable consumers. Because the World Wide Web (WWW) is filled with both accurate and inaccurate information, teachers are obligated to teach K-12 students how to safely access and interpret this information. This chapter addresses issues related to the evaluation of Web pages as well as how to integrate online activities such as Web Quests into your teaching. Web Quests are online scavenger hunts that allow teachers to filter information from the WWW for safe viewing by targeted student audiences. The lesson plans promote safe consumerism by encouraging the use of public domain Web sites for the purpose of creating physical activity engagement.

In chapter 6 the teacher skill set progresses from navigating and searching to developing content for the Internet. Teachers are challenged to create their own Web pages as professional portfolios. These portfolios contain artifacts that offer evidence of the professional growth of new teachers through the use of freeware, such as Mozilla Composer. Strategies for Web development and sequential recommendations are provided for planning and content organization.

Chapter 7 helps teachers refine their word processing skills by creating business cards and student awards and certificates. K-12 students can use word processing skills to create physical activity calendars and make their own Web pages promoting physical activity. This chapter focuses specifically on the advanced features of word processing software such as word count, reading level, and formatting shortcuts. These features, when working properly, make teaching and learning easier and more efficient. The use of templates for enhancing instruction or parental advocacy is also discussed in this chapter.

Chapter 8 introduces desktop publishing for the purposes of advocacy and public relations. Teachers learn how to use Microsoft Publisher to create banners and brochures to communicate with parents and connect with students' lives beyond physical education. Desktop publishing is a unique way to describe policies, procedures, and routines. Students can use desktop publishing to identify community opportunities or materials for use during physical education.

Chapter 9 introduces the use of technology for advocacy through the creation of newsletters. In the first module, teachers create newsletters containing the happenings of the school's physical education program that can be distributed to students and parents in the local community. A newsletter should identify the teacher's philosophy, goals and objectives, standards, and expectations. In the second teacher module, teachers write letters to local businesses to advocate for increased time for physical education classes based on Internet searches that show that adolescents need daily physical activity periods. The lesson plans are for the student media specialist to inform others in their class and school about the success of the sport education team and general highlights from that particular sport season. This promotes the program as well as provides an authentic enactment of the role of media specialist.

Chapters 10, 11, and 12 focus on digital still and video images. In chapter 10, teachers learn how to capture and edit digital images. Chapter 11 addresses the use of Microsoft PowerPoint to create presentations or task cards. Advanced editing and multimedia productions are the focus of chapter 12. K-12 lesson plans in these chapters help students understand movement concepts, work collaboratively, assess themselves and their peers using still and video images, and conduct interviews.

Chapter 13 reviews physical education software and considers its application and integration into the gymnasium setting. This chapter helps teachers evaluate software and make decisions regarding its integration. Teachers are also asked to create lesson plans that incorporate the use of Bonnie's Fitware software for a volleyball unit for secondary students. The student users play the role of the coach and design practice and training plans. The students are also exposed to content about health-related fitness concepts.

Handheld devices provide additional resources and store information gathered from the field. Chapter 14 discusses various handheld devices and formats. Teachers learn to collect performance and observational assessment data with handheld devices, whereas students use them to understand healthy choices and movement principles.

Physical activity measurements are the focal point of chapter 15. Heart rate monitors and pedometers are valuable tools for tracking student progress toward physical activity goals. By helping students calculate the number of steps taken, distance traveled, intensity of exercise, and caloric expenditure, teachers can personalize physical activity instruction. They can also learn about the technology and model behavior for students by assessing themselves. We encourage preservice teachers to implement physical activity measurements into their field experience lessons.

Chapter 16 introduces technologies that have been increasingly incorporated in educational settings, such as blogs, wikis, and podcasts. Each technology is an interactive means of communicating via the WWW. Although teachers are not expected to create or develop these materials themselves, they are introduced to the fact that these technologies are increasingly prevalent. This chapter assists teachers in the design of long-term plans for technology integration. Teachers who have plans to integrate technology on an ongoing basis are those who will remain current because present technologies will soon be obsolete. Continual upgrading and maintenance require creative, well-thought-out planning. This chapter helps teachers plan and meet the demands related to creating and maintaining technology-savvy classrooms.

Because we could not plan for every context or learning situation, a companion Web site is included with editable Word files so that teacher educators can print the modules directly or modify the documents to meet the needs of preservice teachers. Teacher educators or self-taught teachers can also use the modules for their own practice and edification. Teacher educators should not simply use these modules as a cookbook for a technology class; rather, the modules should serve as a guide for the technology that is accessible in their unique contexts. For this reason, each module is general enough to be customized to a specific software or technology. Current physical education teachers should be sure to edit any materials they plan to distribute to their students. Teacher educators and physical education teachers can edit the modules and lesson plans to particular sets of instructions relevant to their laboratory or school settings.

The field experience is a valuable time for future teachers to refine teacher behaviors. It is also a time to use technology with K-12 learners. The K-12 lesson plans and student worksheets provide duplicable activities that can be integrated into field experiences with a minimal amount of planning. Again, teachers should select lesson plans and worksheets relevant to their contexts. Attempting to use these materials in a school that does not have physical education software in its computer lab would result in frustration for both teachers and students. The majority of public schools in the United States, however, are hardwired for use of the Internet, and many even contain wireless capabilities. Therefore, almost every school has some type of technology.

SUMMARY

Technology is here to stay, and it is a permanent part of the teaching and learning process. Teachers have a responsibility to use technologies that enhance student learning and increase teacher efficiency. Children and adolescents need to be taught how to make healthy choices related to technology. For example, using an iPod to motivate a runner or deliver a podcast on training principles is a positive example of technology integration.

In contrast, some teachers use technology simply to amuse or entertain students. This is called *edutainment*. Examples include the use of video games like Dance, Dance, Revolution (DDR) without effective teaching strategies. In edutainment, learning and pedagogy are secondary outcomes to student entertainment. However, some teachers in the United Kingdom have supported edutainment as a way to stimulate specific cultural attitudes. Yet at this point, little evidence exists to show that edutainment enhances student achievement.

This textbook provides many activities to promote learning and physical activity through the integration of technology. Additionally, each teacher activity is designed to provide artifacts for the professional portfolio.

Supportive Materials on the Companion Web Site

The companion Web site (www.HumanKinetics.com/PhysicalEducationTechnologyPlaybook) is home to many files and handouts available for editing and printing. The files have been named to help you identify what kind of file it is.

▶ TM—Teacher Module. A teacher module provides information and also real-world applications that will allow the user to explore technology uses within the classroom.

– *Worksheets.* Worksheets within the teacher modules help guide the learner through the module as well as provide examples of the applications at work.

▶ LP—Lesson Plan. A lesson plan is a guide to help teachers use technology with students in kindergarten through twelfth grade.

– *Student Instructions.* A set of instructions that go along with a lesson plan. These can be handed out to students to follow along as they complete the task and include assessment criteria.

– *Worksheets.* Worksheets within the lesson plans contain further information and working space the students may need to complete the task.

Number	Name	National standards	Materials	Files available
Teacher Module 3.1	Nutrition Analysis	National Standards for Beginning Physical Education Teachers—1	– Internet connectivity – Computer workstations – Completed food logs	– TM03.1 – TM03.1Worksheet (Nutrition Log Sheet)
Teacher Module 3.2	Fitnessgram/ Activitygram Data Entry	National Standards for Beginning Physical Education Teachers—7, 9	– Sit-and-reach box – Mats – Fitnessgram/ Activitygram software – Scale – Tape measure – Data collection forms	– TM03.2
Lesson Plan 3.1 (grades 6-12)	Activitygram	National Physical Education Standards—3, 4	– Laptops – Activitygram software – Student Activitygram worksheets	– LP03.1 – LP03.1Student_ Instructions
Lesson Plan 3.2 (grades 8-12)	Fitnessgram/ Activitygram Goal Setting	National Physical Education Standards—3, 4	– Fitnessgram/ Activitygram report of each student's scores – Paper and pencil or Microsoft Excel	– LP03.2 – LP03.2Student_ Instructions

Number	Name	National standards	Materials	Files available
Teacher Module 4.1	Plotting Heart Rates	National Standards for Beginning Physical Education Teachers—5	– Stopwatch or clock – Computer workstations – Microsoft Excel software – Data collection forms	– TM04.1 – TM04.1Worksheet (Plotting Heart Rates)
Teacher Module 4.2	DataStudio and Probeware	National Standards for Beginning Physical Education Teachers—7, 9	– DataStudio Lite (trial version) – DataStudio USB heart rate sensor	– TM04.2
Lesson Plan 4.1 (grades 6-8)	DataStudio	National Physical Education Standards—2, 4	– Stopwatch or clock – Computer workstations – DataStudio Lite (trial version) – Data collection forms	– LP04.1 – LP04.1Student_ Instructions
Teacher Module 5.1	Web Page Evaluation	National Standards for Beginning Physical Education Teachers—9	– Computer workstations – Internet connectivity	– TM05.1 – TM05.1Worksheet (Top 10 Reasons to Use a Web Site)
Teacher Module 5.2	Designing Web Quests	National Standards for Beginning Physical Education Teachers—1, 5	– Computer workstations – Internet connectivity	– TM05.2
Lesson Plan 5.1 (grades K-2)	Integrated Web Quest: Creating a New Game	National Physical Education Standards—5	– Computer workstations – Internet connectivity	– LP05.1 – LP05.1Student_ Instructions
Lesson Plan 5.2 (grades 9-12)	Drug Czar	National Physical Education Standards—5	– Computer workstations – Internet connectivity	– LP05.2 – LP05.2Student_ Instructions
Teacher Module 6.1	Web Pages as a Professional Portfolio	National Standards for Beginning Physical Education Teachers—5, 8	– Computer workstations – Internet connectivity – Any HTML editing software	– TM06.1
Teacher Module 6.2	Web Development	National Standards for Beginning Physical Education Teachers—3, 5	– Computer workstations – Internet connectivity	– TM06.2 – TM06.2Worksheet (Storyboard)
Lesson Plan 6.1 (grades 6-8)	Creating a New Game	National Physical Education Standards—3	– Computer workstations or laptops – Internet connectivity	– LP06.1 – LP06.1Student_ Instructions – LP06.1Worksheet (Your Game)
Lesson Plan 6.2 (grades 6-8)	Physical Activity in Your Town	National Physical Education Standards—3	– Computer workstations or laptops – Internet connectivity	– LP06.2 – LP06.2Student_ Instructions

CONTINUED

Supportive Materials on the Companion Web Site

Number	Name	National standards	Materials	Files available
Teacher Module 7.1	Business Cards	National Standards for Beginning Physical Education Teachers—9, 10	– Computer workstations	– TM07.1
Teacher Module 7.2	Sport Education Awards	National Standards for Beginning Physical Education Teachers—4	– Computer workstations	– TM07.2 – TM07.2Worksheet1 (Badminton Champions) – TM07.2Worksheet2 (Most Spirited) – TM07.2Worksheet3 (Good Sporting Behavior Award)
Lesson Plan 7.1 (grades 8-12)	Microsoft Word Web Pages	National Physical Education Standards—2, 6	– Computer workstations – Internet connectivity	– LP07.1 – LP07.1Student_ Instructions
Lesson Plan 7.2 (grades 4-5)	Activity Calendar	National Physical Education Standards—6	– Computer workstations – Internet connectivity – Printer	– LP07.2 – LP07.2Student_ Instructions – LP07.2Worksheet (Sample April 2017 Calendar)
Teacher Module 8.1	Public Relations	National Standards for Beginning Physical Education Teachers—9	– Computer workstations – Color printer	– TM08.1
Teacher Module 8.2	Parent Night Information	National Standards for Beginning Physical Education Teachers—5, 10	– Computer workstations – Color printer – Microsoft Publisher	– TM08.2
Lesson Plan 8.1 (grades 9-12)	Banner for a Sport Education Season	National Physical Education Standards—5, 6	– Computer workstations – Color and banner printer – Microsoft Publisher	– LP08.1 – LP08.1Student_ Instructions
Lesson Plan 8.2 (grades 9-12)	Redesigning Recreation	National Physical Education Standards—6	– Computer workstations – Color printer – Internet connectivity	– LP08.2 – LP08.2Student_ Instructions
Teacher Module 9.1	Program Newsletter	National Standards for Beginning Physical Education Teachers—4, 5	– Computer workstations – Printer – Internet connectivity	– TM09.1
Teacher Module 9.2	Letter to Local Businesses	National Standards for Beginning Physical Education Teachers—10	– Computer workstations – Printer – Stamps – Envelopes – Internet connectivity	– TM09.2
Lesson Plan 9.1 (grades 9-12)	Sports Reporting for Newsletter	National Physical Education Standards—2	– Computer workstations – Printer – Microsoft Publisher or Word	– LP09.1 – LP09.1Student_ Instructions
Lesson Plan 9.2 (grades 6-12)	Letter to School Administrator	National Physical Education Standards—5	– Computer workstations – Printer	– LP09.2 – LP09.2Student_ Instructions

Number	Name	National standards	Materials	Files available
Teacher Module 10.1	Reciprocal Teaching Assessment	National Standards for Beginning Physical Education Teachers—8	– Digital video cameras – Batteries – CDs or tapes – Tripods – Extension cords – Microphone (optional)	– TM10.1
Teacher Module 10.2	Digital Assessment	National Standards for Beginning Physical Education Teachers—2	– Digital video cameras – DVD-R recorder – RCA or firewire cables	– TM10.2
Lesson Plan 10.1 (grades 9-12)	Digital Still Assessment	National Physical Education Standards—1	– Computer workstations – Digital cameras – Firewire cable	– LP10.1 – LP10.1Student_ Instructions
Lesson Plan 10.2 (grades 4-8)	Illustrating an Understanding of Movement Concepts	National Physical Education Standards—1, 2	– Computer workstations – Firewire cable – Digital still cameras	– LP10.2 – LP10.2Student_ Instructions
Teacher Module 11.1	Content Knowledge	National Standards for Beginning Physical Education Teachers—1, 6	– Computer workstations – Microsoft PowerPoint	– TM11.1
Teacher Module 11.2	Motor Skill Instruction Project	National Standards for Beginning Physical Education Teachers—5, 7	– Computer workstations – Digital still cameras – Digital video cameras – Microsoft PowerPoint – CD-R or CD-R/W	– TM11.2
Lesson Plan 11.1 (grades 9-10)	Inspector Graphic	National Physical Education Standards—2, 4	– Computer workstations – Digital still cameras – Microsoft PowerPoint – Results from a fitness test such as Fitnessgram/ Activitygram	– LP11.1 – LP11.1Student_ Instructions
Lesson Plan 11.2 (grades 3-5)	There Is No "I" in TEAM	National Physical Education Standards—5, 6	– Computer workstations – Microsoft PowerPoint – Printer	– LP11.2 – LP11.2Student_ Instructions
Teacher Module 12.1	Digital Storytelling	National Standards for Beginning Physical Education Teachers—8	– Computer workstations – Digital video cameras – Microphones – Headphones (optional) – Firewire cables – Windows Movie Maker software	– TM12.1
Teacher Module 12.2	Virtual Gym	National Standards for Beginning Physical Education Teachers—6, 7, 9	– Computer workstations – Digital video cameras – DVD/CD player or laptop – LCD projector – Extension cord	– TM12.2
Lesson Plan 12.1 (grades 9-12)	Digital Storytelling	National Physical Education Standards—5, 6	– Computer workstations – Digital video cameras – Movie Maker, found on all Windows 2000 and later	– LP12.1 – LP12.1Student_ Instructions – LP12.1Worksheet (Storyboard)
Lesson Plan 12.2 (grades 9-12)	Student-Created Virtual Gym	National Physical Education Standards—1, 2	– Computer workstations – Digital video cameras – Firewire cables – Microphones (optional)	– LP12.2 – LP12.2Student_ Instructions

CONTINUED

Supportive Materials on the Companion Web Site   CONTINUED

Number	Name	National standards	Materials	Files available
Teacher Module 13.1	Software Evaluation	National Standards for Beginning Physical Education Teachers—6, 9	– Computer workstations – Software	– TM13.1 – TM13.1Worksheet (Software Evaluation)
Teacher Module 13.2	Volleyball Complete	National Standards for Beginning Physical Education Teachers—6, 9	– Computer workstations – Physical education specific software	– TM13.2
Lesson Plan 13.1 (grades 9-12)	Sim Athlete	National Physical Education Standards—1, 2, 4	– Computer workstations – Sim Athlete software	– LP13.1 – LP13.1Student_ Instructions
Lesson Plan 13.2 (grades 6-8)	Health-Related Fitness	National Physical Education Standards—2	– Computer workstations – Health-Related Fitness software	– LP13.2 – LP13.2Student_ Instructions
Teacher Module 14.1	Documents to Go: Storing Observational Data	National Standards for Beginning Physical Education Teachers—7	– Computer workstations – PDAs – HotSync interfaces – Documents to Go Software	– TM14.1 – TM14.1Worksheet1 (Daily Behavior Rating for Physical Education) – TM14.1Worksheet2 (Daily Behavior Rating for Physical Education [Excel]) – TM14.1Worksheet3 (High School Soccer Rubric [Excel]) – TM14.1Worksheet4 (High School Soccer Rubric [Excel])
Teacher Module 14.2	Teacher Observational Systems	National Standards for Beginning Physical Education Teachers—9	– Computer workstations – PDAs – HotSync interfaces – GoObserve 1.0	– TM14.2
Lesson Plan 14.1 (grades 4-6)	Cooties	National Physical Education Standards—4	– PDAs – Cooties software	– LP14.1 – LP14.1Student_ Instructions
Lesson Plan 14.2 (grades 6-8)	Sketchy	National Physical Education Standards—1, 2	– PDAs – Sketchy software	– LP14.2 – LP14.2Student_ Instructions
Teacher Module 15.1	Pedometers	National Standards for Beginning Physical Education Teachers—2, 6, 10	– Computer workstations – Pedometers	– TM15.1
Teacher Module 15.2	Heart Rate Monitors	National Standards for Beginning Physical Education Teachers—2, 6, 10	– Computer workstations – Polar heart rate monitors – Computer interfaces	– TM15.2
Lesson Plan 15.1 (grades 4-6)	Pedometers	National Physical Education Standards—3	– Pedometers – Miler's Club log sheet	– LP15.1 – LP15.1Student_ Instructions
Lesson Plan 15.2 (grades 6-12)	Heart Rate Monitors	National Physical Education Standards—3	– Computer workstations – Polar heart rate monitors – Computer interfaces	– LP15.2 – LP15.2 Student_ Instructions

Acknowledgments

A special thanks to Lauren Madawick for her module "debugging" and technology expertise. Without her, this book would not have been possible. Many thanks to Anne Gibbone for her imagination and perseverance with initial field testing of technology materials. Additional thanks to Dr. Shannon Whalen for her early pioneering efforts with many of these materials in the computer lab.

Thanks to all of our teachers and coaches who made contributions to this book: David Ascolani, Phil Church, Marie Gregory, Katie Heinrichs, and Erin Nordmeyer.

And finally, thanks to the families that supported our efforts to create this project. We love you all (Logan, Kendel, Brian, and Abby).

Technology as a Means of Enhancing Physical Activity

Physical inactivity and the media are contributory factors to public health issues such as childhood obesity and type 2 diabetes. Specifically, the advances of technology have led to increased screen time (the combination of computer use and television watching) and a reduction in physical activity among children, thus placing them at greater risk for health problems.

Technology is embedded in our society and manifests in our daily actions and behaviors in both positive and negative ways. The development of tools such as cell phones and other communication devices allows us to regularly communicate with those who are important to us as well as to have access to necessary information at our fingertips. However, technology is defined more broadly than tools, machines, devices, or hardware. How we adapt our methodology based on the evolution of the tools is also considered technology. Therefore, technology is both a process and a product (Lynn, Castelli, Werner & Cone, 2007). Because of the evolution of the Internet, we do things differently. For example, we may go to the Internet to obtain information (i.e., learning content, stock reports, national news, or the time the local restaurant opens) and then act on an informed decision opposed to making an educated guess. In the educational setting, teachers can share lesson plans or creative activities, purchase equipment, or join chat rooms to discuss current issues. In general, technology as both a process and product has resulted in the development of technology-rich classrooms that are more motivational to students than those using only traditional methods of instruction. Yet not all contributions of technology have been positive.

Our society and culture have unintentionally discouraged physical activity by introducing new technologies such as electronic games and by reducing the amount of physical activity offered during the school day (U.S. Department of Education, 2000; U.S. Department of Health and Human Services, 2000). Recent studies indicate that many children are physically inactive, resulting in increased health concerns. This inactivity contributes to public health issues such as childhood obesity. Specifically, television, video games, and computers have changed the way we live, including our frequency of physical activity. Ninety-eight percent of all households have at least one television, which is turned on for an average of six hours per day. Even more worrisome is the fact that recent studies have suggested that combined video and computer game usage time exceeds television viewing time (Christakis, Ebel, Rivara & Zimmerman, 2004).

The use of media negatively influences the rate of participation in physical activity because most technology use requires little caloric expenditure. Additionally, television viewing is negatively correlated with physical activity (Marshall, Biddle, Gorely, Cameron & Murdey, 2004). A 2005 Kaiser Foundation study provided evidence that excessive use of media was associated with high levels of discontent among children (e.g., unhappiness, boredom, not getting along well with parents). Also, children with access to electronic media in their bedrooms are likely to have higher viewing hours.

The American Pediatric Association and the American College of Sports Medicine recommend that parents limit the television viewing of children to less than two hours per day. Parents who enforce television viewing rules have been successful in reducing the amount of their children's sedentary time.

In the United States, 9 million children and adolescents are considered overweight (Hedley et al., 2004). In a cross-sectional study that controlled for socioeconomic status (SES) and IQ, overweight children were found to have significantly lower math and reading scores compared to children who were not overweight (Datar, Sturm & Magnabosco, 2004). Furthermore, overweight children often become overweight adults and are less likely to do well in school than those who are physically fit and active (Castelli, Hillman, Buck & Erwin, 2007). Also, school-age children who are unfit may experience serious health problems as they progress through the life span (Fontaine, Redden, Wang, Westfall & Allison, 2003). Some studies have even suggested that children who reached school age in 2000 may be the first generation not to have a longer life expectancy than their parents (Gordon-Larsen, Nelson & Popkin, 2004).

The purpose of this book is to promote the integration of technology into the physical education teaching/learning environment as a means of encouraging healthy physical activity choices among physical education teachers and students. Technology can help to reduce the frequency of sedentary behaviors by allowing students and teachers to assess students' physical fitness and monitor their progress toward personal goals, help students refine their motor skills, comprehend new concepts, and increase their enjoyment of physical activity. Teachers play a valuable role in the selection and integration of technology. Students who know how to use technology to promote and gain an understanding of key concepts related to physical activity, as opposed to those who use technology exclusively for sedentary entertainment, will benefit greatly.

TEACHER PREPARATION AND TECHNOLOGY

To obtain teacher certification, regardless of the subject matter, a person must provide evidence of the attainment of specific technology skills. The International Society for Technology in Education (ISTE) has created technology standards for teachers and students. Other associations, such as the National Council for Accreditation of Teacher Education (NCATE) and the National Association for Sport and Physical Education (NASPE), look to ISTE to set their own guidelines for teacher technology integration. These standards are usually adopted or adapted from those created by ISTE.

Since 2002, all teachers have been required to demonstrate basic competencies in technology use prior to the attainment of teacher certification. Teachers have a variety of technology skills and knowledge and often have been self- or recently taught. Those who have been in the field of physical education for more than five years most likely did not have access to or receive formal training in the technologies presented in this book. Those teachers without technology experience and expertise need to acquire skills in and a level of comfort with advanced technologies, as well as a pedagogical understanding of how to implement technology effectively to foster student learning.

Although computers have been around since the 1940s, the Internet has been a public entity only since 1994, when we begin to rely on personal computers as a means of communication. The amount of information on the World Wide Web (WWW) has grown exponentially, making it difficult to remember life without it. The ever-changing structure of technology products, the burden of remaining technologically current, and the lag in teacher professional development have inhibited the integration

National Standards for Beginning Physical Education Teachers

[as established by the National Association for Sport and Physical Education]

▶ *Standard 1 Content Knowledge.* Understand physical education content and disciplinary concepts related to the development of a physically educated person.

▶ *Standard 2 Growth and Development.* Understand how individuals learn and develop, and provide opportunities that support physical, cognitive, social, and emotional development.

▶ *Standard 3 Diverse Learners.* Understand how individuals differ in their approaches to learning and create appropriate instruction adapted to these differences.

▶ *Standard 4 Management and Motivation.* Use and have an understanding of individual and group motivation and behavior to create a safe learning environment that encourages positive social interaction, active engagement in learning, and self-motivation.

▶ *Standard 5 Communication.* Use knowledge of effective verbal, nonverbal, and media communication techniques to enhance learning and engagement in physical education settings.

▶ *Standard 6 Planning and Instruction.* Understand the importance of planning developmentally appropriate instructional units to foster the development of a physically educated person.

▶ *Standard 7 Student Assessment.* Understand and use the varied types of assessment and their contribution to the overall program and the development of the physical, cognitive, social, and emotional domains.

▶ *Standard 8 Reflection.* Understand the importance of being a reflective practitioner and its contribution to overall professional development and actively seek opportunities to sustain professional growth.

▶ *Standard 9 Technology.* Use information technology to enhance learning and personal and professional productivity.

▶ *Standard 10 Collaboration.* Understand the necessity of fostering collaborative relationships with colleagues, parents/guardians, and community agencies to support the development of a physically educated person.

National Standards for Beginning Physical Education Teachers, 2nd ed. (2003) reprinted with permission from the National Association for Sport and Physical Education (NASPE), 1900 Association Drive, Reston, VA 20191-1599.

National Standards for Physical Education (K-12 Students)

[as established by the National Association for Sport and Physical Education]

Physical activity is critical to the development and maintenance of good health. The goal of physical education is to develop physically educated individuals who have the knowledge, skills, and confidence to enjoy a lifetime of healthful physical activity.

A physically educated person:

▶ *Standard 1:* Demonstrates competency in motor skills and movement patterns needed to perform a variety of physical activities.

▶ *Standard 2:* Demonstrates understanding of movement concepts, principles, strategies, and tactics as they apply to the learning and performance of physical activities.

▶ *Standard 3:* Participates regularly in physical activity.

▶ *Standard 4:* Achieves and maintains a health-enhancing level of physical fitness.

▶ *Standard 5:* Exhibits responsible personal and social behavior that respects self and others in physical activity settings.

▶ *Standard 6:* Values physical activity for health, enjoyment, challenge, self-expression, and/or social interaction.

Moving into the Future: National Standards for Physical Education, 2nd ed. (2004) reprinted with permission from the National Association for Sport and Physical Education (NASPE), 1900 Association Drive, Reston, VA 20191-1599.

of technology into educational programs. Despite these issues, many youth are technologically savvy and motivated by its presence.

SUMMARY

Technology is both a process and a product that has adversely and positively affected physical activity engagement in youth. This book focuses on refining teacher technology skills with the intent to enhance student motivation and physical activity during and beyond the physical education class setting. The teacher learning modules are aligned with specific standards for beginning teachers which produce ideal artifacts for use in portfolios. This book also contains K-12 student lesson plans that are also standards based and developed in relation to factors associated with healthy behaviors.

What Does Technology-Rich Physical Education Look Like?

The middle school students in Mrs. Hisher's physical education class are running with heart rate monitors on, videotaping their performance on a volleyball skill test, dancing to a Dance, Dance, Revolution (DDR) challenge, and assessing their own fitness using the TriFIT equipment. The year is 2008, and it has become a reality that effective instruction in physical education includes the integration of technology. Mrs. Hisher has been teaching middle school physical education for 26 years. Her undergraduate training did not include any experience with today's technologies. To remain current, she regularly takes classes pointing to best teaching practices; however, when it came to technology, she taught herself, one technology at a time. After a school district in-service presentation by a science teacher on data collection in life science, she began to wonder why her students were not analyzing their own fitness and motor skill data. Her story is one of success and perseverance; it took self-motivation to learn the necessary skills, become comfortable enough with each technology to integrate it into her lessons, and find creative ways of obtaining equipment. Her classroom is rich with technology, facilitating student learning and the attainment of the national and state physical education standards.

TECHNOLOGY STANDARDS FOR TEACHERS

The integration of technology into the educational setting has helped to foster teacher learning and facilitate students' problem solving, scientific inquiry, and communication skills. Technology has also helped to advance learning theories and instructional practice. Yet a lack of technology skills among teachers, a lack of funding, accessibility issues, and the ever-changing nature of technology have slowed the comprehensive integration of technology into the educational setting. Governing bodies such as the National Association for Sport and Physical Education (NASPE) and the International Society for Technology in Education (ISTE) have identified essential experiences for teacher preparation that include the attainment of specific standards related to the use of technology. An ISTE initiative funded by the U.S. Department of Education's Preparing Tomorrow's Teachers to Use Technology (PT3) grant program resulted in the publication of the National Educational Technology Standards for all Teachers (NETS-T). The purpose of these efforts was to advocate for the appropriate use of technology in educational settings to improve student learning as well as teacher efficiency.

The ISTE standards have a multipronged focus that includes teacher attainment of skills, the integration of technology to enhance learning, assessment, teacher efficiency, and the ethical issues related to technology (International Society for Technology in Education & U.S. Department of Education, 2003). The NCATE/NASPE standards (located in chapter 1) identify the minimum competencies that all teachers should exhibit within an instructional environment. Specifically related to physical education, NASPE has recommended that programs in physical education teacher education produce physical education teachers who "use information technology to enhance learning and to enhance personal and professional

productivity" (National Association for Sport and Physical Education [NASPE], 2001). The intent of this standard is to ensure that teacher candidates develop a knowledge of and ability to implement current technologies in order to enhance student learning.

To integrate technology effectively, teachers must have the skill and comfort level to do so (Freidus & Grose, 1998). Self-confidence and a willingness to change are also closely related to teachers' use of technology in education (Marcinkiewicz, 1993). Because teachers still feel unprepared to integrate technology into teaching, the most common use of technology continues to be improving teacher efficiency, not facilitating student learning (U.S. Department of Education, 2000). As the accessibility of technology in K-12 schools continues to increase, schools are looking to teacher preparation programs to provide teachers that have the skill and ability to model technology-rich lessons.

TEACHER EDUCATION AND TECHNOLOGY

The National Council for Accreditation of Teacher Education (NCATE) is one of the organizations responsible for providing accreditation of teacher preparation programs and is the agency most frequently used to achieve national accreditation by higher education institutions. ISTE is the professional education organization responsible for recommending guidelines for accreditation to NCATE for teacher preparation programs in computing and technology. All institutions that seek NCATE accreditation must demonstrate how their teacher preparation programs adhere to the ISTE guidelines. This formalized approach to a holistic accreditation process using standards set by field-based experts is based on needs assessments, market needs, and identified effective teaching practices. Despite research-based consensus on what technology standards a beginning teacher should possess, there is little consensus regarding how technology courses in teacher preparation programs should be structured.

The design of technology courses has changed over the years. Initial attempts at teaching technology resulted in direct, teacher-centered methods; focused on the use of computers (Beck, 2000); and were driven by preservice teachers' selection of a college major (Liu, Reed & Phillips, 1990). However, because separate, generic technology courses are unlikely to result in technology integration after employment, technology should be embedded in traditional core courses as typically required at institutions of higher education. A survey of 88 Holmes group education institutions revealed that technology education for teachers was primarily conducted in single courses and lab demonstration formats (Hargrave & Hsu, 2000). Despite the prevalence of single courses in teacher education, other forms of technology integration have evolved to include technology infusion (Morley, 1999), student performance assessment (Jones & Garrahy, 2001; Senne & Rikard, 2002), and case-based integration (Gillingham & Topper, 1999). To date, the use of alternative formats of technology integration into teacher education has been limited.

Essentially, teachers learn how to use and integrate technology into their teaching in three ways: *(1)* They teach themselves, *(2)* they take formal technology classes, or *(3)* they learn from teacher preparation programs that infuse technology into the curriculum. At this point, many technology users in schools are self-taught. Some teachers report having integrated the Internet into their teaching curricula because they enjoy using this technology and consider themselves competent users of the Internet. This is important: Teachers who are comfortable with technology, regardless of how they learned their skills, are the most likely to integrate that technology into their teaching (Freidus & Grose, 1998).

Formal Technology Classes

Technology classes frequently contain learners with a variety of experiences and technological competencies. Class participants range from inexperienced beginners to self-taught learners who are expanding their knowledge to former computer science majors. Take a Web design class, for example. Such a course may contain people who have only visited Web sites, as well as people who are already maintaining their own Web sites but

want to learn specific design features. This diversity of learners makes it difficult to organize and instruct a technology course that meets the needs of all learners.

The format and effectiveness of technology courses in teacher preparation programs have not kept pace with the availability of technology for K-12 schools (National Center for Education Statistics [NCES], 2000), yet first-year teachers are expected to integrate technology into their lessons (National Association for Sport and Physical Education [NASPE], 2001). According to the National Center for Education Statistics, only 20% of teachers report feeling well prepared to integrate technology into teaching (National Center for Education Statistics, 1999). Teacher preparation programs need to address the problem of incorporating technology into daily practice (Sandholtz, 2001).

Although most teacher educators agree that specific teaching and learning activities need to be integrated into technology courses, some institutions offer only a "survey" of technologies. Common topics in technology courses include multimedia, problem-solving applications, networking, the Internet, software evaluation, telecommunications, and hypermedia (Abdal-Haqq, 1995; Baron & Goldman, 1994; Taylor & Weibe, 1994). This content and the single-course format may lead to mastery of basic computer skills, but they do not result in continued growth and implementation during employment (Lagone, Wissick, Langone & Ross, 1998), thus highlighting the limitations of the single-course format.

A study examining small groups of special education program graduates confirmed the limitations of a single technology course: Beginning teachers lacked continued technology growth upon employment in K-12 educational settings (Lagone, Wissick, Langone & Ross, 1998). Despite initial changes in the attitudes and skills of the teachers, institutional barriers impeded a continuation of or progress toward technology integration. These findings suggest the need to examine the structure of instructional technology courses. They also call for the sustained support of and the provision of current materials to new teachers.

Over time there has been a shift toward the use of more subject matter–specific instruction focusing on media and teaching strategies (Hargrave & Hsu, 2000). The content addressed in a single technology course should be applicable to the teaching of specific subject matter and the uniqueness of the instructional setting. In this textbook, chapters 3 through 16 specifically address this issue by providing subject matter–specific activities. Particularly, we provide activities for the teacher-learner as well as the student-learner so that both can gain a better understanding of how to use technology in the physical education setting.

Technology Infused In Teacher Preparation Programs

Since involvement in creating authentic projects has the potential to change preservice teachers' perceptions about technology integration, teacher education programs should look carefully at their systematic efforts to improve preservice teachers' attitudes through curricular reform in an effort to plan for preservice teachers who are student centered and confident in their abilities to teach and to integrate technology into the curriculum (Stuhlmann, 1998). For example, preservice teachers experience an instructional technology course that focuses on providing hands-on experience in order to obtain the necessary skills and knowledge specifically identified by the ISTE. The culminating experience was the presentation of student Web-folios. In this class experience, preservice teachers had to demonstrate their growth and development by creating and maintaining online portfolios containing media and documents as evidence of their professionalism. When the preservice teachers then enter the K-12 school sites, they can design a similar technology-rich experience for their students with confidence about the end results.

Because most future teachers do not use technology during their field experiences and do not work with cooperating teachers and supervisors who can advise them in technology use (Moursund & Bielefeldt, 1999), it becomes the responsibility of teacher educators to train and provide application opportunities for preservice teachers throughout their educational experiences. Some teacher education programs require preservice teachers to experience technology in several courses. For example, a class may require a student to create a PowerPoint presentation. In another example, preservice teachers may be required to videotape their teaching in an early field experience. These examples do not teach teachers how to integrate the specific technology, but they do help them refine their personal technology skills. However, because a teacher's level of comfort with technology is the primary barrier to technology integration (Freidus & Grose, 1998), the infusion of technology across a developmentally appropriate sequence of classes is most effective.

When technology is effectively infused across the curriculum, learners are not only refining their technology skills, but also simultaneously increasing their pedagogical knowledge. In one study examining change in classroom practice, computers were identified as a means for providing new constructs in pedagogical knowledge (Dexter, Anderson & Becker, 1999). Since teacher preparation institutions have had this information since 1999, there should be ample opportunities for pedagogical knowledge to be constructed in a supportive climate, thus providing evidence of best practice first and effective integration of technology second.

Faculty often use technology for communication and information gathering but not to instruct others in the use of technology. A lack of research in instructional technology makes faculty hesitant to invest time in creating technology-rich assignments for preservice teachers. Technology training for teachers has also been limited by the lack of skills of faculty members and the fact that technology skills are often discussed but not necessarily practiced (Lonergan, 2001).

Despite debate regarding how technology should be taught to preservice teachers, many agree that teacher education programs should integrate technology simply because it is part of today's society. An effective technology course can help teachers more efficiently use their time in a variety of tasks such as the following:

▶ Monitoring student progress

▶ Maintaining student portfolios

▶ Preparing classroom materials

▶ Communicating with students, parents, and administrators

▶ Exchanging ideas and curricular materials with other teachers

▶ Consulting with experts in the field

▶ Accessing remote databases

▶ Further expanding teacher knowledge and professionalism

A single technology course provides only one way future teachers can become comfortable with technology. Regardless of the format, it is imperative that the integration of technology be purposeful. Because the knowledge, skills, and technology that classify literacy are always changing, future teachers need basic technology literacy as well as the ability to develop, apply, and evaluate technology-based instructional materials for educational use.

TRAITS OF TECHNOLOGY-SAVVY TEACHERS

Exemplary technology-savvy teachers are different from other teachers. These teachers use more details when describing the classroom setting, select instruction carefully, and interact with a network of other technology-savvy teachers. Like effective teachers in general, technology-savvy teachers use comprehensive descriptors to explain their classrooms (Castelli & Rink, 2003; Ertmer, Gopalakrishnan & Ross, 2001). For instance, exemplary technology-savvy teachers use teaching and learning goals more than non-technology-using teachers do to describe their instruction. These teachers "can express why students performed well on the performance indicators [standards] because their actions are purposeful attempts to attain student competence" (Castelli & Rink, p. 529). Unlike non-technology-using teachers, these teachers believe that they have an obligation to prepare their students for the future (Gillingham & Topper, 1999).

Similar to other exemplary teachers, technology-savvy teachers use strategies from across the instructional style continuum. They embrace a variety of instructional styles to address student learning and adjust their instructional practices to meet student needs and content. As suggested by Castelli and Fiorentino (2004), the content in physical education teacher technology courses determines the appropriateness of the instructional methods, because technology is an extension of their teaching. One example shows how technology can help to address negative perceptions associated with assessment (Mohnsen, 2008; Worrell, Evans-Fletcher & Kovar, 2002). By providing meaningful, novel, and diverse assessments (Martin, Kulinna & Cothran, 2002), technology-rich teaching motivates students to attend to the task at hand. When technology is used, students focus on the activity and not the assessment.

Teachers who effectively integrate technology ask the following questions during their planning: (1) How will technology improve teacher efficiency? (2) How will the integration of technology foster learning? and (3) How does the technology accomplish something that previously could not be accomplished? These teachers carefully and purposefully consider the learning outcomes first, and then consider how the technology can contribute to the lesson.

Technology can be employed to improve teacher efficiency rather than be an expensive frill. For example, a teacher could use a handheld device to take attendance, store lesson plans, collect assessment data, and monitor student performance. This information, temporarily stored on the handheld device, can be instantaneously transferred into more formal and permanent storage (e.g., spreadsheets and portfolios), thereby addressing the ever-increasing need for help in dealing with paperwork issues (e.g., attendance, grades, assessments). Technology that improves teacher efficiency is teacher centered, because the students have little interaction with the devices.

The integration of technology can also foster student learning by presenting information in a variety of ways. According to Howard Gardner (1997), who has a broad and pragmatic perspective on intelligence, we all learn in different ways. Technology can help address the multiple intelligences of learners by presenting content in the style in which it can be best learned. The student who is most expressive in musical forms might benefit from having music or digital audio and video integrated into the lesson. Those students strong in logical-mathematical intelligence have the capacity to use numbers effectively and therefore may understand the concept of target heart rate better through the use of heart rate monitors.

In each of these examples, the focus of the technology integration is on the learner, not the teacher. Enhanced comprehension of content is thus the intent of using technology. A teacher who integrates Dance, Dance, Revolution (DDR) into a fitness lesson may have the learning objective of increasing students' aerobic capacity; however, to the spatial learner who has enhanced sensitivity to color, lines, shapes, and space, the experience involves much more than simply being physically active. Technology, if thoughtfully integrated to address specific standards of learning, can deepen student learning and help meet a variety of learning objectives.

Technology can help achieve goals that may have been difficult to attain in an earlier era. For example, teachers watching student performances in real time may have difficulty identifying which critical elements are missing or need to be modified for students to be successful. A digital video can allow students to slow down the speed of their own performances to analyze them. Other technologies, such as the Internet, allow for immediate access to information, media, or direct communication with experts. Digital video as well as the Internet can help students accomplish tasks that may have been considered impossible in a different environment.

For example, an urban student who could not participate in orienteering because it was unsafe and impractical could participate in virtual orienteering via the Internet.

TECHNOLOGY INTEGRATION IN PHYSICAL EDUCATION

According to Roblyer (2003), there is no question about the need for and potential of technology in classrooms in our society of technology adopters (cell phones, automated teller machines). The integration of technology requires new skills for both students and teachers, frequently resulting in greater problem solving, collaboration, and the creation of new knowledge for both groups of users. As with all new technology, the learning curve could be an initial barrier. Future teachers are required to attain mastery of basic computer competencies prior to certification (NASPE, 2001), but some physical education teacher education programs are requiring coursework and competencies beyond those required by mandates. At two institutions, preservice physical education teachers' comfort, ability, and self-efficacy increased with participation in a technology course designed for physical education content (Castelli & Fiorentino, 2004), thus facilitating their integration of technology related to the national physical education standards (NASPE, 2004) upon entry to the field.

Traits of Programs That Use Technology

Physical education teachers from effective programs have regular communication with students and parents; integrate student choice in the curriculum; and link the national standards to student learning (Castelli & Rink, 2003). Technology can play a role in each of these characteristics. Communication can be enhanced through the use of the Internet. Teachers can create Web sites targeting both students and parents that contain policies and procedures, expectations, homework assignments, or newsletters. Technology can also help teachers offer students choices within the curriculum, even within some lessons. For example, in a lesson using learning stations, students may be able to choose from participating in Tae Bo, Virtual Gym, or DDR. Choice, as well as technology, is motivational for students and helps to increase their levels of engagement.

In all educational environments, teachers must link performance standards to practice. Technol-

ogy can help to make this connection. Teachers from effective programs are able to use various forms of technology to collect assessment data and therefore track student attainment of specific benchmarks related to each standard. Technology can help K-12 students achieve state and national physical education standards and also provide teachers with an efficient mechanism to document those achievements.

Teachers in effective technology-rich programs select, master, and integrate one technology at a time, all the while working within their own levels of comfort and knowledge. It is unreasonable to assume after reading this chapter—or the entire text—that a teacher should be able or willing to integrate all of the technologies at once. Instead, teachers should select a single technology, plan for the acquisition of the technology, become comfortable with it, and then integrate it into their lessons.

The information regarding technology-savvy physical education teachers and programs is largely in the anecdotal stage. Few studies have focused specifically on how much technology has helped to enhance teacher efficiency or foster student learning. The important thing that teachers must remember is that technology should not be integrated unless teacher efficiency or student learning is enhanced. At this point, it does not seem to matter how teachers acquire technology skills and improve their personal comfort levels; it is more important that they possess the technology skills prior to introducing the technology into the teaching environment.

SUMMARY

Technology-savvy teachers teach differently than non-technology-using teachers do. This is in part due to the new information and perspective that the technology provides. The effectiveness of technology integration is a direct result of teachers' skills, comfort levels, and abilities as well as their establishment of classroom rules, routines, and procedures. Technology can enhance student learning and facilitate (and document) the achievement of the national physical education standards. Integration of any new course materials or curricula may be inhibited by contextual issues such as resistant teachers, budget limitations, or issues related to time. Yet, the time to integrate technology is now, not when the issues magically disappear. Any integration of technology will take time and effort because change is not a single event but a product of many.

Data Entry: As Simple as One, Two, Three

student steps off of the scale located in the locker room and says, "How much should I weigh?" You point to the chart on the wall and state that the body mass index provides an indication of the appropriateness of his weight relative to his height. You also add that his nutritional habits may influence his weight. "Remember, body weight is just one way to measure body composition; skin folds, underwater weighing, and bioelectrical impedance are others. Your body weight will vary as you grow and develop, particularly now during middle school. It is funny that you should ask about body weight, because today in class we will be collecting height and weight information and entering it into the Fitnessgram/ Activitygram software. We will also spend some time discussing body composition and nutrition."

In the vignette, the student presented an interesting question that the teacher was well prepared to answer. Timely, accurate responses to anatomical and physiological questions are the obligation of the physical education teacher. Teachers in all educational settings need to be able to process a rapidly growing amount of information. **Data entry** and information processing help teachers and students ensure the smooth and efficient handling of information. After typing text or numerical data into a computer, the student can analyze information in a way that was impossible without the integration of technology. This chapter addresses NASPE teaching standards 1 (content knowledge), 7 (student assessment), and 9 (technology) through a discussion of data entry and the use of spreadsheets.

DATA ENTRY

Data entry is the process of entering distinct pieces of information organized by categories into a computerized **database** or **spreadsheet**. This can be performed by a person typing at a keyboard or by a machine entering data electronically (e.g., the infrared beam on a cash register that reads the bar code on a box of cereal). This chapter focuses on how teachers and students can enter data into computers or software programs for enhancing learning. In some instances, these data are converted, whereas in others the computer performs very little analysis. The simplest kind of data entry consists merely of pointing at something, selecting an item, or designating a position on a computer monitor (e.g., in the Activitygram software), whereas in more complicated modes of data entry, a user may have to control the format of storage as well as its contents.

Following are some data entry programs:

- ▶ Microsoft Excel
- ▶ Fitnessgram
- ▶ Activitygram
- ▶ Nutrition Analysis Tools (NAT)

Physical education teachers enter data into computers, calculators, spreadsheets, and various software programs to evaluate student performance, assign grades, determine levels of fitness, or analyze efficiency of movement. Physical education teachers should be proficient at entering data for two reasons: *(1)* It will increase their productivity, and *(2)* it will allow them and their students to access information that might not otherwise be available in the educational setting. For example, the Fitnessgram/Activitygram software can convert a student's personal information (gender, age, height, weight) into a body mass index (BMI) score. The software is also capable of producing a report that identifies whether the BMI is in the healthy fitness zone or needs improvement. It is important to remember that some data inputs can initiate or interrupt information transactions (e.g., entering a specific number or data item might open a new window that requests additional input, or entering the data and then asking for an "analysis" will present the analysis outcome rather than a list of the entered data). Others simply display the information in its original form.

FORMAT CONTROL

Before using software that requires data entry, a physical education teacher should consider the **format control**, which is the means of data entry. Data entry can be completed through text editing, text entry, or graphic interaction. With text entry, the teacher uses a keyboard to enter the data (e.g., a Microsoft Excel spreadsheet or a calculator). Text editing data entry requires using drop-down lists or information that is already on the screen and linking it to the student identity (e.g., the Nutrition Analysis Tools and System Web site). Graphic interaction is like a video game in that the person selects an icon or graph to represent a piece of information being saved into the database.

A format control that requires teachers to type all of the data into the database themselves could become an inhibitor if teachers are responsible for hundreds of students at a time. In other software programs, the data can be networked from other sources (e.g., Fitnessgram/Activitygram version 8.0). For example, the names and birth dates of the students could be taken from the school district's database, thus reducing the amount of information the teacher needs to type into the database. The teacher must thoughtfully consider the format control before initiating data entry.

In one format, a user might enter numbers, letters, or more extended textual material by keying or, in some applications, by speaking. These data could be entered directly into displayed forms, tables or constrained message formats, or appear as free text. If a graphic interaction format is used for data entry, users might draw pictures or manipulate displayed graphic elements, such as data entry into tablet-style laptops. The various types of data entry all merit consideration here.

THE SYSTEM: WHERE WILL THESE DATA GO?

The computer, or the permanent storage location, will also play a role in the data entry process. Some software and hardware will guide users who need help, check data entries to detect errors, and provide other kinds of data processing aids, whereas others will not. Interface software designers must be concerned about computer processing logic as well as data input and the skill level of the user. The consumer must review the key features of the software, the system requirements for its use, the amount of storage space, the interactive format or mechanism by which the data are entered, and the limitations of both the hardware and software.

Most software applications have more features than the normal user will ever use; therefore, it is important that the user identify the features that are most important for the specified task. For example, a teacher may want to use both a school computer and a home computer to conduct the data entry. This means that the teacher will need to import and export these data on occasion. Depending on the software you use, data can be exported as tab delimited, as comma delimited, or in a format that is unique to the software, so it is important for the teacher to be familiar with the specific means for exporting data. Additionally, some software will have "debuggers," which note inaccuracies in the data entry and then notify the user that the information is illogical. For instance, Fitnessgram/Activitygram will notify a teacher if the entered date of birth is inappropriate for a student in a specified grade. The user should first identify the features that are available within a price range, prioritize the features that are needed, and then question the functionality of the features. Finally, prior to purchasing or installing software on a computer, the user should confirm that the system requirements match or exceed those required.

Some statistical analysis packages are so complex that they can produce a **terabyte** of information from multiple-level analyses. It is therefore important that the user determine how much storage is available and how much the software package requires. Typically, a handheld device will hold up to 20 megabytes of information. A teacher who needs more than this would need to purchase a memory card. Table 3.1 displays the equivalency of various file sizes. Despite the fact that external storage space and memory card prices have dropped substantially, it does mean one more purchase out of an already limited budget.

Many laptops are designed to use a touchpad and button system for data entry, which often results in slower data entry when compared to a traditional mouse and keyboard. Unlike desktop computers, tablet-style laptops often save data as picture files (e.g., JPEG), which may not be as easily transferable into other programs used for quantitative analysis unless converted by additional software. Many hardware devices now can use infrared beams that are convenient and quick, but data are sometimes lost in the transfer. Teachers must consider the most efficient way to

TABLE 3.1 File Size Equivalency

8 bits = 1 byte				
1,000 bytes	1 kilobyte (K)			
10,000 bytes	10K			
100,000 bytes	100K			
1,000,000 bytes	1,000K	1 megabyte (MB)		
10,000,000 bytes	10,000K	10MB		
100,000,000 bytes	100,000K	100MB		
1,000,000,000 bytes	1,000,000K	1,000MB	1 gigabyte (GB)	
1,000,000,000,000 bytes	1,000,000,000K	1,000,000MB	1,000GB	1 terabyte (TB)

enter data for their purposes and then purchase software that makes the most sense for their teaching environments.

A frequently noted problem with data entry devices and software is the duplication of input. Teachers should seek out programs that allow them to draw from preexisting databases (e.g., school enrollment data and school attendance) to avoid having to reenter information. The teacher must obtain the specifications of the **interface** (programming the computer) to maintain the context within which the preexisting data bases are configured. Thus, when a teacher identifies a student name, via a network, the computer program should be able to access all previously entered data that is relevant and not require the teacher to enter such data again.

To enhance their efficiency, teachers can maintain data such as student performance scores, attendance records, and evidence of social responsibility. These data can be entered manually into a spreadsheet or database for conversion or interpretation. The most common or practical use is producing student grade reports. Yet, noted in the following chapters, the data can also serve as advocacy discussion items, as guidance for teacher planning (extending or refining student tasks), or to accept student feedback about task performances. Databases can enhance student learning by providing new information. Timely, congruent feedback about performance (e.g., motor skills, tactical decision making, and frequency of socially responsible behavior) can play a major role in keeping students focused on specific task components, in turn promoting consistency. Specifically, by entering fitness test scores into the Fitnessgram/Activitygram software, a student can develop goals based on personal strengths and weaknesses. This individualization of instruction enhances student learning.

SUMMARY

Despite the time commitment required for data entry, the information revealed through converted, transformed, or interpreted data has the potential to enhance teacher efficiency and student learning. The number of laps completed on the PACER test alone provides little valuable information to the learner. Yet, using the Fitnessgram/Activitygram software, teachers can track the progress of students toward fitness and educational goals and improve their comprehension levels. Teacher modules and lesson plans in this chapter and chapter 4 require the entry of data through multiple formats to be used in authentic contexts, such as the one described in the vignette at the beginning of this chapter.

LEARNING MODULES

The learning modules are available to download from the companion Web site at www.HumanKinetics.com/PhysicalEducationTechnologyPlaybook.

Teacher Module 3.1 Nutrition Analysis

In the first teacher module, teachers analyze their nutritional habits through the process of data entry. Using a diet recall format, teachers enter personal food intake over a one-week period. This requires that they reflect on their nutritional habits as well as attempt to modify their diets. The changes in their behavior are tracked and confirmed by recording food intake over a two-week period. After recalling food intake, teachers enter data into a nutritional analysis program that converts the data to generate new information. Teachers are asked to reflect on the process of attempting to change their personal nutritional habits. Online data entry programs are valuable for use in schools, sport programs, sport industry environments, and fitness sites.

Completing this task should give teachers enough relevant background to help them use other similar online data entry programs to analyze personal data. The rationale for this assignment is to encourage teachers to reflect on their personal caloric intake and positions as role models, as well as to consider recreating this assignment for students (or other target audiences).

Teacher Module 3.1 Nutrition Analysis is available to download from the companion Web site.

Teacher Module 3.2 Fitnessgram/Activitygram Data Entry

In the second teacher module, teachers administer Fitnessgram/Activitygram assessments to K-12 students as part of a comprehensive battery to measure physical fitness. (Teachers who do not have access to K-12 students may administer the Fitnessgram/Activitygram assessments to each other.) Teachers select and administer five assessments, then enter the K-12 student scores into the Fitnessgram/Activitygram software. Each teacher must complete the data entry and print a copy of the Fitnessgram/Activitygram report relative to the personal data entered for each of the K-12 students.

This module reiterates the importance of specific adherence to the testing protocol in order to obtain valid and reliable data on the student fitness reports. Teachers need to be competent administrators of Fitnessgram/Activitygram to K-12 students, which is unlike administering the assessment to adults. In actual school settings, teachers need to be able

Teacher Module 3.2 Fitnessgram/Activitygram Data Entry is available to download from the companion Web site.

to accurately collect information about the fitness levels of K-12 students, enter data into an analysis program, and print out reports with suggestions for improvement. Teachers who learn to use the Fitnessgram/Activitygram software can extend its use outside of school sites—for example, to sport camps and health clubs.

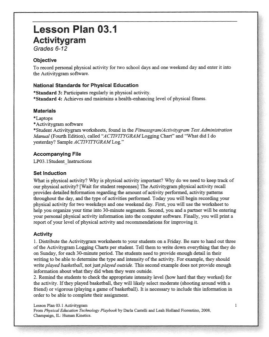

Lesson Plan 3.1 Activitygram is available to download from the companion Web site.

Lesson Plan 3.1 Activitygram

The student Activitygram module requires students to record their physical activity for two weekdays and one weekend day into the computer software. The software is organized in half-hour increments, so students can use a handout to prompt accurate recall of their physical activity levels. Students will also generate printable reports, which they will be encouraged to take home. The most important feature of this module for teachers is the interpretation of the data to assist in decision making for curricular or instructional design, or both. For example, if the students in a specific class have low levels of physical activity outside of school, their teacher could identify healthy alternatives within the community or even plan a field trip to a local facility to familiarize students with accessible physical activity sites.

This module calls student attention to personal physical activity levels and provides an opportunity for students to critically analyze their level of physical activity. It is intended that through this analysis, students will come to better understand the importance of physical activity and its role in disease prevention. Students will also be able to make comparisons between their weekday and weekend levels of physical activity.

Lesson Plan 3.2 Fitnessgram/Activitygram Goal Setting

This learning module should be completed in two phases; the first is through completion of the series of fitness tests from Fitnessgram/Activitygram. The second phase, which the module focuses on, requires students to interpret their Fitnessgram/Activitygram reports and develop two personal goals related to their health-related fitness. For example, a student might state, "to increase my cardiorespiratory endurance and the number of laps completed on the PACER test from 15 to 22, getting me into the Healthy Fitness Zone." The student is then required to develop a personal physical activity plan to enact both during and beyond physical education class to achieve the goal. This module is valuable because it helps students understand the importance of attaining and maintaining physical fitness as well as allowing them to choose how to accomplish their goals.

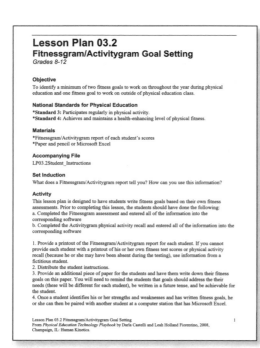

Lesson Plan 3.2 Fitnessgram/Activitygram Goal Setting is available to download from the companion Web site.

Charts and Graphs: Plotting a Course for Success

There is a buzz in the air because the first schoolwide "gym show," called Circus Skills, is scheduled for this evening. You have worked very hard to get your students prepared to juggle scarves, spin plates, and balance on unicycles. You are also well aware that this evening is not simply to display the talents and abilities of your students; it is also a time for advocacy. Your efforts to provide learning experiences that maximize participation have wiped out your budget. You want to expand the offerings within your curriculum, which means more equipment. Tonight is the ideal time to ask for more money; however, you feel compelled to provide evidence for why you need it. To summarize your students' learning and display their progress, you take scores from rating scales and enter them into Microsoft Excel. You then import the data into Microsoft PowerPoint and make several charts and graphs, by activity and grade, to present to the audience after the show.

This chapter addresses NASPE standards 5 (communication), 7 (student assessment), and 9 (technology). Specifically, we discuss how charts, graphs, and spreadsheets can help facilitate communication about student performance.

SPREADSHEETS

A spreadsheet is a table that shows data in rows and columns. Microsoft Excel, a software program built around spreadsheet functions, allows the user to enter data into a spreadsheet and subsequently manipulate the data. The spreadsheet is one of the most popular uses of the personal computer, and often this software is included in the purchase of a computer.

Spreadsheets were originally used by accountants to organize and display data about business transactions, because data arranged in rows and columns are easily analyzed. Once entered into the spreadsheet, data can then be added to give a total, or sum. A spreadsheet software program summarizes information from many paper sources in one place and presents the information in a format to help a decision maker see the "big picture."

The most logical application of spreadsheets in teaching is student grade reports. Teachers must track student progress toward specific learning goals, and this can be done quickly and efficiently using a spreadsheet. By nature, the spreadsheet is customizable to meet the needs of each teacher. For example, a spreadsheet containing various mathematical functions can accommodate both a teacher who uses weighted grades and one who uses a total point system.

In Microsoft Excel, to begin using a spreadsheet, select *File*, then *New File*. On the screen are preformatted columns and rows, forming cells. The user should title the columns and rows before beginning data entry. In a Microsoft Excel spreadsheet, data are typed into the cells, as opposed to being imported using an infrared device. Once the spreadsheet has been created, users can insert functions (such as calculating the sum of numbers in a column or the percentage of adjacent columns) or create charts and graphs for their data. Users must remember to save their work frequently while entering data to avoid any loss of pertinent information as a result of adjusting to different software functions.

CHARTS AND GRAPHS

Charts are organized by placing information on the y axis (the value axis) and x axis (the category axis). As you learned in chapter 3, some software quickly converts data into reports or unique displays. Microsoft Excel contains spreadsheets that simply require the user to enter data into the cells (by specific column and row) to display on the chart. The user can manually create the chart by selecting the chart type, range, criteria, and other related features. The user also has the option of using an on-screen wizard, which does allow for choices; however, the software completes the majority of the work. Teachers are not limited to using only Microsoft Excel; many graphing calculators now allow users to enter, store, and display data in the form of charts and graphs. The modules in this chapter require students to collect their own heart data, store it using DataStudio or Microsoft Excel software, and then graphically display these data.

Charts also may include a title, a legend, or axis subtitles. The title should be brief (one or two words) and articulate the subject of the information being displayed. For example, in the vignette at the opening of this chapter, the teacher might display a chart that shows how the number of student catches has improved over time. The title may read, "Catches Over Time," or "Now We Can Juggle!" A legend identifies the color, pattern, or symbols that represent data on the chart. The type of chart determines the nature of the characters representing the data. The axis subtitles help the reader understand the purpose of the data.

Types of Charts

Common types of charts are line, area, column, bar, pie, doughnut, radar, and scatter plots. The line chart is used for showing how data change over a specific interval. For example, in the opening vignette the teacher may want to display how many catches were made by each class. If she has conducted weekly application tasks (i.e., a form of assessment) requiring the students to record the number of catches, she could display the data on a line chart or bar chart. Table 4.1 is a chart depicting the number of catches students made during their best attempts at juggling on five consecutive Fridays.

TABLE 4.1 Number of Student Catches Reported Over One Month

	CATCHES				
Date	8/25/2008	9/1/2008	9/8/2008	9/15/2008	9/22/2008
Student 1	2	4	7	12	12
Student 2	1	5	8	13	17
Student 3	3	6	9	14	18
Student 4	6	8	1	25	19
Student 5	4	11	0	13	20
Student 6	10	12	11	15	22
Student 7	3	6	12	17	50
Student 8	4	8	13	9	30
Student 9	1	4	14	10	39
Student 10	6	6	8	13	27
Student 11	3	5	9	14	15
Student 12	2	7	10	15	28
Student 13	1	3	4	16	31
Student 14	2	4	8	10	25
Student 15	8	5	12	9	36
Student 16	3	7	11	13	24
Student 17	2	5	13	14	12
Student 18	5	8	9	17	28
Student 19	6	9	10	20	33
Student 20	2	11	11	25	44
Class average	3.7	6.7	9	14.7	26.5

The students worked in pairs, one juggler and one recorder. Only the best score for the day was given to the teacher. Using a handheld device (see chapter 14), the teacher electronically stored the information in a table or spreadsheet. In the final row of the spreadsheet (see table 4.1), the average number of catches for the entire class was automatically calculated.

The data from the spreadsheet were used to create a line chart and a bar chart. The line chart (see figure 4.1) includes the scores of the first five students and tracks their progress over time. Notice that the x axis (category) identifies the trial

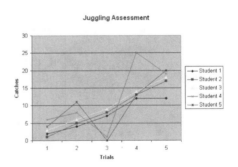

Figure 4.1 Line chart of individual juggling catches.

number, and the *y* axis (value) identifies the number of catches made by the student across five assessments of juggling. Although the chart is valuable, it seems busy and cluttered. The audience may get lost in the complexity of the chart, which may lessen its impact. The second chart (figure 4.2), a bar chart, displays the class average over time, not the performance of all 20 students. The use of averages allows for simultaneous representation of all students; however, it is limited because it does not reflect the range of performance.

Area charts are similar to line and bar charts in that they show the amount of change over time. Each line represents an assessment, and the area below the line is filled with a color or pattern (see figure 4.3). This allows for direct comparisons between data points by determining whether there is an increase or decrease in the amount of area above and below the data point.

Scatter plots are useful for showing the relationship between two or more data series (i.e., juggling assessments) at uneven intervals. In figure 4.3, the teacher assessed the number of catches for juggling one time each week. Teachers who can conduct assessments only irregularly can benefit from the use of scatter plots (see figure 4.4).

Unlike line, column, bar, and area charts, pie and doughnut charts show the relationship of the data recorded in table 4.2 to the whole (see figure 4.5). A pie chart is useful for showing the relationships between factors. Because it can show only one data series (i.e., one assessment), a pie chart would not be appropriate for the juggling example. However, a pie chart would be appropriate for displaying how funds were generated and allocated for the purchase of new juggling equipment.

Charts or graphs can also include pictures or graphics such as cones, cylinders, arrows, and stars (see figure 4.6).

Why Use a Chart or Graph?

We have already noted that charts and graphs are important for advocacy in physical education programs. However, displays of this type can also

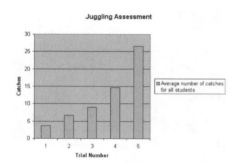

Figure 4.2 Bar chart of class average for juggling catches.

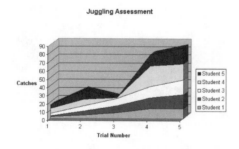

Figure 4.3 Area chart of individual juggling catches.

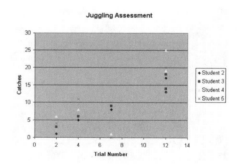

Figure 4.4 Scatter plot of individual juggling catches.

TABLE 4.2 Cost of New Juggling Equipment

Parents	School	Fund-raisers	Other	Total cost
400	1,000	400	200	2,000

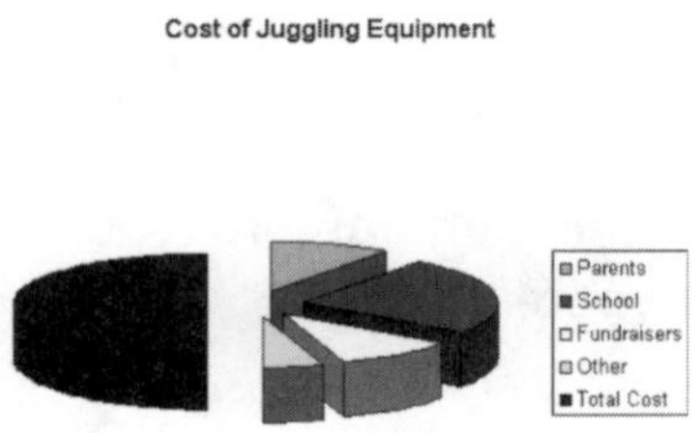

Cost of Juggling Equipment

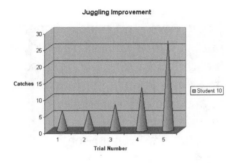

Figure 4.5 Pie chart of contributions to the purchase of juggling equipment.

Juggling Improvement

Figure 4.6 Cone chart comparing student improvement in juggling.

serve physical education students. Charts and graphs can be used to *(1)* monitor student progress toward personal or group learning goals, *(2)* motivate students, and *(3)* display information about the group. Teachers in effective physical education programs monitor student progress (Castelli & Rink, 2003), particularly when attempting to promote regular physical activity. Students whose teachers regularly document and report student performance (e.g., how often, how long, or how hard the students have been physically active; how many steps the students have taken) report being more physically active than those whose teachers do not (Castelli & Rink, 2003). The monitoring of student progress also allows the teacher to unite multiple learning goals, such as physical activity and fitness goals.

Students, with few exceptions, want to meet the expectations of teachers. With the use of charts, teachers can clearly communicate expectations by displaying goals for the class or for individual students. For example, a teacher who wants students to be able to bench press 60% of their body weight by the end of the instructional unit could motivate them by using a pictorial display of their achievements so they can see their progress.

When dealing with the measurement of health-related fitness variables (e.g., body weight, aerobic fitness, number of sit-ups completed), teachers must remember that this information should remain confidential. For example, body weight should never be displayed publicly. To protect the identity of individuals but provide incentive for the students, the teacher can display data on the entire class. A teacher could set a goal for all students in one class period to attempt to lift 500 pounds (227 kg) as a group. This allows for comparisons across classes but protects personal information. In this example, everyone contributes to the goal.

The use of live graphing is valuable for upper elementary school students. Performance data collected using USB sensors or probeware (e.g., heart rate monitors, force plates) can be instantly graphed at the completion of the testing protocols. Students can watch a computer monitor and see their heart rate increase when they jog in place as opposed to standing or sitting. Live graphing allows students to adjust their performance to match an ideal graph. For example, to learn which jump rope skills expend the most energy, a student can attempt various jump skills while a peer views the fluctuation in heart rate, force production, or breathing rate. Many life science classes are already using this technology.

SUMMARY

Charts and graphs are effective means of displaying data to communicate student progress toward specific learning goals and to motivate students. There are many ways to display the data, and some are rather complex. Simple charts or graphs, clearly identified by titles and legends, are the most helpful. Teachers with the skills and ability to construct these displays can quickly communicate distinct messages to varied audiences. Teachers who are proficient in the use of technology can produce charts and graphs to communicate their expectations to students as well as to assess student performance.

LEARNING MODULES

The learning modules are available to download from the companion Web site at www.HumanKinetics.com/PhysicalEducationTechnologyPlaybook.

Teacher Module 04.1
Plotting Heart Rates

Objective
To record heart rates after different activities and then use Microsoft Excel to create a graph displaying these heart rates.

National Standards for Beginning Physical Education Teachers
Standard 5 Communication. Use knowledge of effective verbal, nonverbal, and media communication techniques to enhance learning and engagement in physical education settings.

Materials
*Stopwatch or clock
*Computer workstations
*Microsoft Excel software
*Data collection forms

Accompanying File
TM04.1 Worksheet (Plotting Heart Rates)

Discussion Question
What are some of the advantages and disadvantages of teachers using software, such as Fitnessgram/Activitygram or Grade Book, that requires a high volume of data entry?

Directions
1. You will take your heart rate nine times during three different physical activity conditions for a 10-second period.
   a. *Resting*: At rest, count the number of heartbeats in 10 seconds and multiply by 6 to have your heart rate in beats per minute (bpm). Save the information on the worksheet (TM04.1 Worksheet) in the appropriate space.
   b. *Activity 1* (light physical): Three times during the two minutes of your light physical activity (e.g., easy walking), you will stop and take your heart rate for 10 seconds. Multiply that number by 6 and save that information on the worksheet in the appropriate space.
   c. *Activity 2* (vigorous physical): Three times during the two minutes of vigorous activity (e.g., jumping), you will stop and take your heart rate for 10 seconds. Multiply that number by 6 and save that information on the worksheet in the appropriate space.
2. Enter the recorded heart rates into an Excel spreadsheet.

Entering Heart Rates Into a Spreadsheet
1. Microsoft Excel spreadsheets are made up of cells. A cell is where a row and column meet. Because Microsoft Excel is cell specific, information needs to be entered correctly and accurately (see figure 4.1).

Teacher Module 04.1 Plotting Heart Rates   1
From *Physical Education Technology Playbook* by Darla Castelli and Leah Holland Fiorentino, 2008, Champaign, IL: Human Kinetics.

Teacher Module 4.1 Plotting Heart Rates is available to download from the companion Web site.

Teacher Module 04.2
DataStudio and Probeware

Objective
To use the DataStudio software and PASCO probes or sensors or heart monitors to collect and analyze heart rate data.

National Standards for Beginning Physical Education Teachers
*Standard 7 Student Assessment.** Understand and use the varied types of assessment and their contribution to the overall program and the development of the physical, cognitive, social, and emotional domains.
*Standard 9 Technology.** Use information technology to enhance learning and personal and professional productivity.

Materials
*DataStudio Lite trial version (free download from www.pasco.com/datastudio/)
*DataStudio USB heart rate sensor

Discussion Questions
*How could a science teacher and a physical education teacher collaborate to help students better understand human physiological responses to physical activity?
*What are some specific projects that students in grades 8 to 12 could complete?

Directions
In order to prepare for this module, it is best to purchase and use the PASCO sensors, but it is not necessary. Free demo software and heart rate data collected using heart rate monitors can be used to collect and compare heart rate data for various physical activity conditions. This module can be completed using heart rate data collected using a traditional measure of pulse or heart rate monitors (see chapter 15) and entered into the DataStudio software, thus eliminating the live graphing feature.
1. Plug the USB connector on the heart rate sensor into the computer to start the software.
2. Select *EZ Screen*.
3. Place the heart rate sensor on your finger, earlobe, or hand between your first finger and thumb.
4. Click the green circle (in the upper left-hand corner) and record the heart rate.
5. After a few seconds, click the red circle in the upper left-hand corner.
6. Remove the heart rate sensor and hand it to your partner.
7. The partner places the heart rate sensor on his or her finger, earlobe, or hand between the first finger and thumb.
8. The partner clicks the green circle (in the upper left-hand corner) and records the heart rate.
9. After a few seconds, the partner clicks the red circle located in the upper left-hand corner.
10. Save your data and your partner's data to your disk.

Teacher Module 04.2 DataStudio and Probeware
From *Physical Education Technology Playbook* by Darla Castelli and Leah Holland Fiorentino, 2008, Champaign, IL: Human Kinetics.   1

Teacher Module 4.2 DataStudio and Probeware is available to download from the companion Web site.

Teacher Module 4.1   Plotting Heart Rates

In the first teacher module, the objective is to enhance teachers' knowledge of using media as a means of communication. Specifically, teachers record and report their personal heart rates during three physical activity conditions, then use Microsoft Excel to create a spreadsheet and graphic display of the data. Teachers palpate their radial or carotid pulse using their index and middle fingers to determine their resting heart rate and heart rates during selected activities, thus allowing for direct comparison of heart rate data across the three conditions. Teachers are held accountable for the accuracy of their data entry and the appropriateness of their charts.

This module prepares teachers to use Microsoft Excel for more than just grades. This assignment requires teachers to display information in a graphic illustration, thus presenting the information in a form that K-12 students can easily understand. Teachers will be able to transfer written records of their heart rates into personalized charts to enhance professional presentations. They may also use the charts they generate as visual aids to supplement oral communications of their results to students, parents, administrators, or other professionals.

Teacher Module 4.2   DataStudio and Probeware

The second teacher module reinforces similar concepts using various software and data collection tools. The DataStudio software is commonly used in technology-rich science curricula. This software uses PASCO sensors (e.g., heart rate monitors, motion detectors, or force plates) to collect information regarding performance outcomes. The ideal way for a physical education teacher to enact this module is to collaborate with a science teacher by having students collect data during physical education class and analyze the information during science class. This comprehensive approach to learning promotes critical thinking, the scientific process, and the application of findings to an authentic situation. A trial, or Lite, version of DataStudio can be downloaded for free (www.pasco.com/datastudio); using data entry techniques (discussed in chapter 3), any numeric data can be analyzed. However, a PASCO sensor must be purchased to create a graph while data are collected.

The DataStudio software promotes data collection and analysis using probeware and comes in two formats, Lite and Full. The Lite version is sufficient for the purpose of these modules and can be downloaded for a free 90-day trial. This software contains the basic tools for importing, displaying, and analyzing data. This software can be used as a stand-alone product or in conjunction with specific probeware. Probeware are sensors, such as heart rate monitors, motion detectors, and force plates, that are compatible with USB ports and allow anyone to collect and store information gathered in the field.

The purpose of teacher module 4.2 is to inform teachers about software and hardware devices that might be useful in a collaborative partnership with science educators. Teachers across various subject areas can create projects in which students enact experiments and collect data in the gymnasium, then analyze the data and give them meaning later in a science class. In this case, students could use the results to design personal physical activity programs based on their needs.

Lesson Plan 4.1 DataStudio

Both teacher and student learning modules in this chapter require the measurement of heart rate within a physical activity setting and the use of software to create an illustration of these data to track progress toward personal or group goals.

Similar to teachers, students collect, analyze, and display data by typing them in or using a PASCO sensor to collect them. The interpretation of the data will lead to practical applications for personal health status and physical activity patterns.

To complete this module, students enter the DataStudio software and are greeted by four icons: (1) *Open Activity,* (2) *Create an Experiment,* (3) *Enter Data,* and (4) *Graph Equation.* It is immediately apparent that the software and probeware are typically used in science education. Yet the collection of human biological data, such as physiological responses to various exercise intensities, would make for an ideal collaborative project. Options 1 *(Open Activity)* and 2 *(Create an Experiment)* require the full version of the

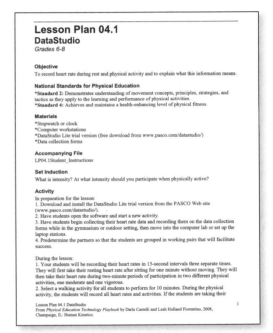

Lesson Plan 4.1 DataStudio is available to download from the companion Web site.

software as well as the use of probeware. Using the data entry portion of the software, the user then enters the heart rate data into the software by denoting which data point belongs on the *x* axis (category) and which belongs on the *y* axis (value). Then the software, similar to Microsoft Excel, allows the user to make decisions about how to display the data. The resulting chart or graph is printable.

Navigating the Web as a Knowledgeable Consumer

While sitting at your computer on Sunday afternoon, you begin to search the World Wide Web (WWW) for health-related fitness terms, such as *muscular strength,* in preparation for a health-related lesson you will be teaching. Unfortunately, during your Google search, you find that not all of the information is current, accurate, or safe to access. Specifically, you discover lots of inaccuracies about heavy weight training practices for children and adolescents, which, according to the American College of Sports Medicine (ACSM), are contraindicated. You decide that, rather than simply lecture students in the classroom, you would prefer that they work through a Web Quest in the computer lab. You go to www.teachnology.com and begin to construct a Web Quest for your students to complete. After the lesson, the students report being highly motivated because they liked doing something new as well as working in pairs.

As suggested in the preceding vignette, this chapter addresses NASPE standards 1 (content knowledge), 5 (communication), and 9 (technology). Unlike chapter 4, which addressed technologies that enhance communication through the display of student performance scores, this chapter addresses the use of the Internet to access information such as lesson plans, findings from research studies, and class activities. You will be taught to use a keen eye and critical evaluation skills as a knowledgeable consumer of information.

The Internet has been around since 1962, but it was not until the expansion of the **World Wide Web (WWW)** and the development of Mosaic in 1994 that these technologies became household items. Initially, the **Internet**, an electronic network of computers, was used only by the U.S. military to exchange information. The notion of connectedness then expanded to university libraries looking to conduct interlibrary loans with greater efficiency. Unbeknownst to some people, the Internet is not synonymous with the WWW; the Internet represents only the network of computers and servers that are linked. The Internet globally connects the information systems by linking computers through **Transmission Control Protocol/Internet Protocol (TCP/IP)** computer addresses. The WWW is the medium that is used to share the information across the Internet, through hypertext markup language (**HTML**) or **JavaScript,** to name a couple.

The contents and capability of the WWW have grown exponentially since 1994, as a result of contributions to the network, the addition of servers, the creation of new forms of **Web browsers** (e.g., Internet Explorer, Netscape, Mozilla Firefox, and Opera), and the posting of Web content in the form of Wikipedia. The WWW has an endless supply of information that we have come to rely on. Unfortunately, not all of this information is current, accurate, or safe to access.

TELECOMMUNICATION AND THE WORLD WIDE WEB

Telecommunication is any electronic transmission, or the sending and receiving, of information. We frequently think of e-mail as the primary means of telecommunication; however, television, facsimiles, and other media also fall into this category. Telecommunication allows for the expedient and efficient exchange of information. Initially, these communications mandated a hardwired connection, but this is becoming less of a requirement as wireless service is increasingly available to the consumer.

The Internet is a form of telecommunication that can be used to locate information, communicate with others, or display information for others to view. **Web browsing** is considered "wandering," "surfing," or "navigating" the WWW. Browsing happens through the use of Web browsers, or **search engines,** that access information by linking keywords to the text in the titles, descriptions, or contents of Web pages. The Internet user must first select a browser. Each browser has its strengths and weaknesses. For example, Internet Explorer works very well with other Microsoft products; however, because the Internet market includes competitors, compatibility is not always seamless. In addition, some browsers have user options that make them more attractive to the general public. For example, both Netscape Navigator and Mozilla Suite have HTML editors built into the software, which is a noticeable advantage over Internet Explorer. HTML editors allow the consumer not only to navigate, but also to edit or create Web pages without having to know the programming language of HTML.

Once a user has selected a browser, she is now free to roam the WWW. As she discovers information, she may want to **bookmark** a site for future reference. Each browser has a pull-down menu from the top toolbar that allows the user to mark and save the **URL** (Web address) of favorite sites. This makes for faster navigation on return visits to that site, because all the user has to do is select the site from a list of favorites.

WHAT IS A "GOOD" WEB SITE?

Navigation through the WWW and within an individual Web site requires a discriminating and keen eye. Roblyer (2003) created a list of criteria for evaluating a Web site based on site content, visual and audio design, navigation, and other miscellaneous items. This rubric is valuable to both Web page developers and novice Web surfers, such as younger students. Students can be taught to qualify the accuracy of the information within the visited site.

According to Roblyer (2003), the content of a Web site should be up-to-date, with currency denoted by "last updated" on the bottom of the page. Users should be skeptical of sites that lack this information. The content on the Web page should be easy to read and reflective of the type of person who might visit the site. To identify whether a site is friendly for students of a specific grade level, a teacher can use the browser Yahooligans to determine readability and appropriateness. Additionally, Web pages should be free of inappropriate language and subtle stereotyping and bias. The most useful Web sites also provide contact information so the reader can interact with the Web page designer.

Web sites should be graphically appealing and thematic. Pages with an overabundance of graphics are slow loading and often distracting. The first page of the Web site should provide an overview of the site, perhaps even containing a site map or search mechanism. Sites void of these characteristics can be difficult to navigate and, if necessary, reference. All links on the page should be in proper working order. Despite the organic nature of the WWW, broken links generally indicate that the information has not recently been updated.

Finally, the Web surfer needs to be both judge and jury. Some Web sites may meet all of the criteria outlined by Roblyer and yet still not be accurate. For example, Wikipedia is a relatively new phenomenon in which individuals can write reviews or update information contained in this online encyclopedia. Yet, what is posted is not scrutinized by content experts. The information may be littered with opinions or bias rather than based on empirical evidence. Therefore, it becomes the responsibility of the reader to judge the authenticity of the content. Cross-referencing information to confirm its accuracy is a necessary part of Web navigation.

WEB QUESTS

Web Quests, introduced by Bernie Dodge, are a series of interwoven activities that are theoretically grounded in cooperative learning, higher-order thinking, authentic assessment, constructivism, and service learning (Dodge, 2006b). Some have called Web Quests online scavenger hunts that guide students through accurate information previously identified by the designer of the Web Quest. Unlike some teacher-created Web-based activities, Web Quests are purposefully designed to allow students to construct knowledge through efficient and effective Web navigation. Students are not merely surfing for information about the topic, but instead are engaged in sequential steps to obtain new knowledge from accurate online resources.

All educators can use the Web Quest inquiry-based model for teaching subject-matter content. However, what is especially exciting for physical educators is the prospect of connecting students to relevant, timely, and authentic sources as they begin to identify the challenges of healthy living throughout the life span. The Web Quest model makes efficient use of students' time as they use Web-based information and apply higher-order thinking skills in pursuit of realistic solutions to problems. This model effectively integrates activities from the WWW into the classroom. The integration process presents exciting design challenges to teachers and inviting learning challenges to students. The challenge for educators is to control the chaos of the Internet and distinguish between biased opinions and truthful information (Dodge, 2006a).

Another use that has exciting potential for educators is the professional sharing that occurs during the creation of Web Quest materials and the eventual exchange of student work with other student groups and interested expert groups. The beauty of the Web Quest experience comes in the group work that engages the students in the learning process. The increased student interactions are of critical value to the development of cooperative skills. In addition, students have the option of posting their Web Quest projects on the Internet for external reviewer feedback, or simply saving the project and sending it to professionals in the local community, or across the world for an international perspective. The options are unlimited. A number of effective learning theories and strategies are evidenced in this professional sharing, including, but not limited to, critical thinking, cooperative learning, authentic assessment, technology integration, schema theory, scaffolding, and constructivism. These theories and strategies become more important when they are viewed through the perspective of a physical educator's need to motivate students to learn and challenge students to use higher-order thinking skills and work cooperatively with their classmates and across the sharing community (March, 2006a).

A Web Quest is a perfect model for learning because it presents a central question that students can answer by making connections to an authentic situation rather than one specific to the classroom context. Additionally, the Web Quest model increases students' motivation because they receive positive feedback from the external (sharing) community, which can carry greater impact and validation than simple teacher feedback. Students have access to data sources that are current, relevant, and accurate while simultaneously communicating with nationally known researchers and leaders of special-interest groups. The Web Quest model also involves a group process in which contributions from all members are valued and expected. Finally, because the Web Quest group work is shared publicly with other communities, students are motivated to work at a higher level with respect to the quality of the final project (March, 2006b).

PRECAUTIONS

As previously mentioned, using the Internet has a few drawbacks, primarily security. Information can be stolen from personal accounts, from Web pages, or through the input of data (e.g., credit card numbers or Social Security numbers) into unsecured Web sites. To protect personal as well as school computers, firewall security software should be installed and regularly updated. Even though a firewall protects the home or school network from hackers or unwanted communication with individuals outside the network, the software is not 100% foolproof. Internet users should be well educated in the practice of safe computing. For example, secure Web sites are often identified by an *s* as part of the URL (i.e., https://www). Following are safe computing practices:

▶ Install and regularly update security (i.e., firewall), pop-up blocker, spam blocker, and antivirus software.

▶ When using a computer in a public place (e.g., the library), close all programs and windows before leaving the computer.

▶ Know the history and reputation of a Web site before inputting any personal information (e.g., credit card numbers or Social Security numbers). Many secured site include *https* as part of the URL.

▶ Do not download anything from the Internet until you investigate its authenticity.

▶ Use an alias e-mail with a spam blocker to eliminate unwanted messages.

▶ Limit your online enrollment to listservs, blogs, and so on.

SUMMARY

The WWW has great potential, and teachers should be using it to exchange professional information. Teachers are obligated to be educated consumers of the Web and to teach students how to be educated consumers. Web Quests are one way a teacher can provide authentic, safe learning activities that require students to scrutinize the information on the WWW. By filtering the information prior to student viewing and identifying safe contacts, educators can teach students how to use these tools appropriately to enhance their knowledge.

LEARNING MODULES

The learning modules are available to download from the companion Web site at www.HumanKinetics.com/PhysicalEducationTechnologyPlaybook.

Teacher Module 5.1   Web Page Evaluation

In this chapter, the learning modules require that teachers first evaluate content on Web pages and then use this information to construct a Web Quest for use in an instructional setting. Using a popular search engine and a criteria-based evaluation tool, teachers navigate the WWW and evaluate five Web pages that have similar subject-matter content.

Teacher Module 05.1
Web Page Evaluation

Objective
To use a popular search engine and a criteria-based evaluation tool to examine five Web pages containing similar subject matter.

National Standards for Beginning Physical Education Teachers
Standard 9 Technology. Use information technology to enhance learning and personal and professional productivity.

Materials
*Computer workstations
*Internet connectivity

Accompanying File
TM05.1Worksheet (Top 10 Reasons to Use a Web Site)

Discussion Question
How can teachers effectively use the World Wide Web to help students achieve the national physical education standards?

Directions
1. Prior to the beginning of this module, get acquainted with the Web page evaluation criteria.
2. Conduct a Web search on a topic related to your teaching or future employment by using one search engine from the following list that you have never used before.
   *Alta Vista: www.altavista.com
   *Ask Jeeves: www.ask.com
   *Dogpile: www.dogpile.com
   *Excite: www.excite.com
   *Google: www.google.com
   *Lycos: www.lycos.com
   *Yahoo: www.yahoo.com
   *Yahoo!Kids: http://kids.yahoo.com
3. Using the accompanying worksheet (filename: TM05.1Worksheet), select five Web pages from your search and evaluate their content. Rank your pages by the number of criteria that each page met. Identify which of the Web pages are appropriate for a specified target audience that you might be teaching.

Teacher Module 05.1 Web Page Evaluation   1
From *Physical Education Technology Playbook* by Darla Castelli and Leah Holland Fiorentino, 2008, Champaign, IL: Human Kinetics.

Teacher Module 5.1   Web Page Evaluation is available to download from the companion Web site.

Teacher Module 5.2   Designing Web Quests

The second module requires teachers to use some of the "approved" Web sites as resources on their own Web Quests. This module exposes teachers to the basic skills for creating a Web Quest. A free Web site, www.teachnology.com, provides a Web Quest template complete with clipart. The Web Quest can be saved and edited or enhanced by using any HTML editor, such as Microsoft FrontPage, Microsoft Word, or Adobe Dreamweaver. After teachers have created their Web Quests, they should share and critique each other's pages. This module also requires certified teachers to create lesson plans that integrate Web Quests into K-12 physical education.

Teacher Module 05.2
Designing Web Quests

Objective
To create an interactive Web Quest about a topic related to physical activity or physical education.

National Standards for Beginning Physical Education Teachers
*Standard 1 Content Knowledge.** Understand physical education content and disciplinary concepts related to the development of a physically educated person.
*Standard 5 Communication.** Use knowledge of effective verbal, nonverbal, and media communication techniques to enhance learning and engagement in physical education settings.

Materials
*Computer workstations
*Internet connectivity

Discussion Question
What is a Web Quest?

Overview
This module introduces the basics of creating a Web Quest. You will be using a free online program called Teach-nology to help you construct your first Web Quest. You can save your Web Quest as an HTML file and then enhance it by using an HTML-editing program such as Microsoft FrontPage, Microsoft Word, or Adobe Dreamweaver. The following steps will get you started in creating a meaningful and effective Web Quest for your students.

Directions
1. Prior to beginning this module, choose a topic that will be of interest to your target audience and visit a variety of Web sites to determine whether they would be useful for linking to your Web Quest.
2. Visit the following URLs to see Web Quests created by other teachers to get some ideas for your own. These Web Quests are available online for anyone to use.
   *www.ashlandschools.org/mark_sherbow/pbl2-9/smoking.html
   *http://technoteacher.com/WebQuests/index.htm
   *www.geocities.com/whatastich/WebQuestAbstinence.html
   *http://horizon.nmsu.edu/kids/webquests/
3. Visit the following URL: http://teachers.teach-nology.com/web_tools/web_quest/ to begin the creation of your Web Quest.
4. Begin by entering the introductory information in the *Heading* and *Title* section. Try to develop a catchy title for the Web Quest because it helps to capture student interest.
5. Select a picture from the gallery that connects with your topic. If there are no interesting images, try the Microsoft online design gallery.

Teacher Module 05.2 Designing Web Quests   1
From *Physical Education Technology Playbook* by Darla Castelli and Leah Holland Fiorentino, 2008, Champaign, IL: Human Kinetics.

Teacher Module 5.2   Designing Web Quests is available to download from the companion Web site.

Lesson Plan 5.1 Integrated Web Quests is available to download from the companion Web site.

Lesson Plan 5.1 Integrated Web Quest: Creating a New Game

Because of the complexity and sensitivity of the issues related to the use of the Internet, this lesson plan requires students to become knowledgeable Web consumers. In this lesson, students use a preexisting Web Quest to create a new game to be used in physical education. The tasks focus on locomotor and manipulative skills as well as safety for kindergarten through second grade students.

Lesson Plan 5.2 Drug Czar is available to download from the companion Web site.

Lesson Plan 5.2 Drug Czar

The objective of the second lesson plan is for a small group of students to develop a Web Quest addressing the dangers of using a specific performance-enhancing or weight loss drug. Students become experts and share the information with their classmates.

Web Page Development

You are a new elementary physical education teacher in the school district, and it has come to your attention that your expectations may be a little higher than the previous teacher's. Several students have commented, "Mr. Sales didn't do things that way." You see 725 students per week, and you have difficulty remembering what you said to which class because they rotate through the schedule so quickly. You decide that perhaps the best way to make your expectations clear is to create a Web site for parents to visit. Your school district has already provided you with a template and a one-day training session describing how your information and materials can be published to the Internet. Now all you need to do is decide what your Web site will look like and what information it will contain.

Because of its popularity and accessibility, the Internet is a viable means for disseminating information to students, parents, and other teachers. NASPE standards 1 (content knowledge), 5 (communication), and 9 (technology) are addressed in this chapter. Unlike chapter 5, which addressed the Internet as a source of learning, this chapter addresses it as a means of delivering information to both students and parents.

A **Web site** is a collection of **Web pages** linked by a common URL (Web address), or **home page.** Originally, the development and organization of content for upload onto the Internet required a knowledge of codes or scripts. Now anyone can create a Web site because software packages make designing them as simple as point and click.

Why do teachers need to have their own Web sites? The answer is simple. A Web site provides a means of communication with parents, students, administrators, and other teachers while also extending learning beyond the classroom. Today a Web site can be viewed from desktop computers, laptops, and handheld devices (see chapter 14) including cell phones.

Teachers can create simple Web sites to display current information for students and items of interest to the school community. A Web site is an alternative communication format for information typically distributed through posters, flyers, and home mailings. In addition, students can create visually exciting projects or homework on computers and save them on Web sites. Web sites can be viewed on the local computer where it was generated (offline) or be saved and viewed on multiple computer stations.

Parents are also key stakeholders in students' success (Battle-Bailey, 2004). They can become more supportive of the learning process by being informed about teacher expectations, policies, procedures, assignments, and key events. Web sites allow parents to share in their children's learning experiences and reiterate teacher expectations at home.

A teacher's Web site should be practical, unique, and customized to the needs of its target audience. It should adhere to a single purpose and be professionally organized and disseminated. Many of the characteristics of an effective Web site were identified and discussed in chapter 5. The teacher can now move beyond the role of Web site critic and Web Quest designer into more advanced responsibilities related to Web development.

Web development programs come in various formats. Some are designed like word processors, presentation generators, or other primary intents, yet all programs possess the capability to save the materials in a Web-ready format. Software such as Mozilla Suite, Adobe Dreamweaver, Adobe GoLive, and Microsoft Office can be used to create Web sites. Selection of software should be based on the desired type of Web site, the available technology budget, the skills and abilities of the teacher, and the amount of interactivity desired on the site. Teachers should select software prior to designing a Web site to avoid being disappointed by having designed something they cannot create. If budget is an issue, the free downloadable Mozilla Suite may be the best choice. Although it has limits related to formatting (e.g., it does not allow for placing multiple frames of Web pages on a single page), it is highly functional and relatively easy to use. Macromedia Dreamweaver should be selected for more advanced Web development, because this software defines and assists the user in building complex, highly interactive Web sites.

WEB DEVELOPMENT STRATEGIES

In general, Web pages within a Web site should have a consistent look and feel. This may seem like an obvious directive, yet many Web developers disregard it. Multiple resources suggest step-by-step procedures to effective Web development. We are including a list of steps currently used in technology courses based on our experiences. To create a Web page, and ultimately a Web site, we recommend that teachers follow these steps, in order:

1. Determine the type of Web site.

2. Gather information and identify the important content.

3. Chunk the information.

4. Sketch a storyboard.

5. Select a design template.

6. Insert interactive elements.

7. Publish and test the Web page.

Determine the Type of Web Site

There are several types of Web sites, including informational sites, **blogs** (Web logs are discussed in chapter 16), databases, and **wikis** (collaborative Web sites discussed in chapter 16). A Web site may be the work of an individual teacher or a collaborative effort of many teachers. There are also business-oriented, rating, and search engine sites (discussed in chapter 5). The teacher must select which type of site to create. Most common is an informational site, which provides information about a physical education program to a larger audience beyond the school.

After determining the type of Web site, the teacher must identify the purpose of the site and the target audience. A Web page should be content-rich, yet easy to read. This means avoiding pages that have too much text and are too long; in the case of Web sites, less is more. It is best to take a minimalist approach, especially when first designing a Web site. Teachers should employ limited hyperlinks and graphics, except where these items would make significant contributions to learning. Unnecessary features, such as large pictures, slow down the loading speed of the Web page and often distract the user's attention.

Using a word processor, the teacher should create a purpose statement describing the intent of the content that follows. This text will eventually appear on the main menu, or home page, of the Web site. The text should be concise, contain proper mechanics and spelling, and be written at the reading level of the target audience. The teacher can select more than one audience to address, such as parents and students, but the content for each audience should be clearly defined and organized prior to creating the Web site.

Gather Information and Identify the Important Content

Once the physical education teacher has determined the type of Web site and the primary audience, she should gather information related to her purpose. Other relevant Web pages can be used as references, samples, or hyperlinks. For example, the teacher could have a link to the PBS Kids site Maya and Miguel's World of Sports (http://pbskids. org/mayaandmiguel/english/games/sports/). This site explains the history and rules of many sports and provides online games of horseshoes, ping pong, soccer, archery, and boomerang. The text is in kid-friendly language and is delivered in both Spanish and English. This page encourages viewers to try these sports activities on their own time as a way to stay healthy by providing printable rules of the sport activity and game setup. A teacher wanting to increase interaction can add more links to the Web page. However, she must remember that each time a viewer uses a link, he is traveling away from the Web site and may choose not to return.

Other valuable information for the teacher to collect includes images, videos, tables, and other figures. The teacher should keep copyright laws in mind when using the Internet to gather information (see the following Copyright Information sidebar).

During this stage of Web development, the teacher should also develop and gather electronic documents and pictures to be included on the Web site. Depending on the purpose, items such as policies, procedures, field trips, required attire for class participation, teacher expectations, or physical activity challenges could be included. Sometimes parents are unaware of the physical education class schedule and curriculum content, so these are also viable possibilities for including on a Web site. It is best to develop these materials first, perhaps even pilot them as hard copies, before including them on a Web site. For example, a teacher who would like to alert students that digital still or video cameras will be in the classroom should have the media release form approved by

Copyright Information

Briefly, the United States 1976 Copyright Act seeks to protect work (e.g., documents, images, and recordings) originated by people other than the user. Teachers are permitted to use materials authored by others strictly for spontaneous educational purposes. However, taking an image from someone else's Web site, whether clearly identified as copyrighted material or not, and placing it on a personal Web site is illegal. Teachers should author their own materials and images whenever possible. Fair use is influenced by the educational purpose, the amount of material taken from someone else, the uniqueness of the material, and remuneration. Specifically, a teacher could use a video segment of the evening news as a teachable current event for a 10-day period. After that time he would need to destroy the video clip or obtain permission to keep the video. Teachers can examine copyrighted materials for 45 days before being required to secure permissions. The Library of Congress Web site (www.copyright.gov/) has answers to questions about copyrights.

building administrators prior to dissemination. It is important that all gathered materials be stored electronically for easy retrieval (just think of the teacher who suddenly says, "This is my last copy"). Transferring materials to the WWW requires fewer steps and less time when the materials are already in an electronic format (e.g., .doc, .txt, .jpg).

Chunk the Information

Once the majority of information has been gathered and the important concepts identified, the teacher now needs to place these items into categories. Information processing is based on how learners store and interpret knowledge (Massare & Cowan, 2006). Cognitive scientists believe that teachers can assist learners in getting concepts into short-term (and ultimately long-term) memory by presenting information in a way that encourages them to make connections with past experiences. Chunking information, therefore, is a way to organize information into logical "chunks" that are similar and connected to students' past experiences. Cognitive scientists refer to this chunking as schema. In practical terms, chunking also allows users to simply follow directions linking all similar content. The chunks that form this content could be placed on a single page with the user navigating from top to bottom or across different Web pages (the teacher will need to make this decision in the next step).

To more effectively chunk the content, the Web developer should store like information and file formats in a single folder. For example, the developer may want to create a folder titled "Images" in which to store all photos, clipart, and pictures. These folders should all be placed within a single Web site folder to preserve associated links. Files in the Images folder should be saved in a **JPEG** or **GIF** format. (GIF refers to the file name extension .gif, which is for layered images that appear to be in motion. GIFs can make Web sites fun and attractive, yet if overused, they can be distracting and unprofessional.) Images saved during the gathering phase should now be placed in this folder. It is important that teachers protect students by not including images and information that might identify them. Slightly blurring the image is one way to protect students in photographs. As previously discussed, posting of student images to the WWW requires a media release form from the school district administration, which includes consideration for parental permission policies as stipulated by the school district administration.

Teachers need to plan in advance and collect pertinent materials in a central location. This central location is often called a resource folder. In the resource folder the teacher should place a list of the potential URLs that will serve as links, as well as text documents containing contact and school information. Some schools provide this information as part of the district template, whereas at others individual teachers need to collect this information.

Sketch a Storyboard

A home page is the first page that the user sees on a Web site. It should display a purpose and be organized in a menu format. A menu contains a table of contents that includes all information contained on the Web site. From the home page the user should be able to navigate throughout the entire site. The home page should provide enough information for the audience to make wise choices regarding navigation and Web consumerism (see chapter 5). User choice is a valuable characteristic of the home page, but it can easily be overdone and in turn overwhelm the user.

The menu of a Web page needs to be logical and clearly articulate the contents and navigational capabilities of the Web site. The easiest way to do this is to use the categories in which the information was chunked in the previous step. Using the software program Inspiration or a plain piece of paper and pencil, the teacher can sketch the contents of each Web page. Like the author of a comic strip, the teacher uses squares to define what information will appear on the menu versus what will appear on any additional Web pages (see figure 6.1). The software program Inspiration, often used by language arts teachers, helps the designer create a concept map of ideas (see figure 6.2). Because this software is available in many schools, we recommend it for organizing Web site categories.

The storyboard also provides the teacher with an outlet to experiment with colors, fonts, and themes. A teacher will need to decide whether to adhere to school colors or create a unique design template.

Select a Design Template

It is important for the Web developer to create and maintain a consistent format that uses a set background color, font type, and style. Each Web page should contain a toolbar of all the places to navigate within the Web site. The location and format of this

Figure 6.1 Storyboarding your Web page.

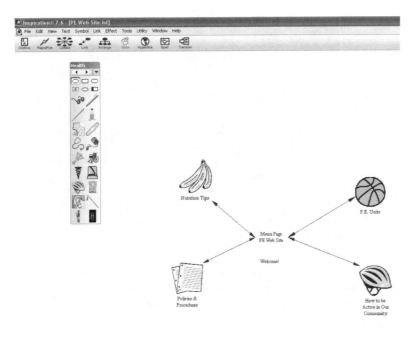

Figure 6.2 Using Inspiration to design Web pages.

Diagram created in Inspiration® by Inspiration Software®, Inc.

toolbar should be consistent across all Web pages (see figures 6.3 and 6.4 on page 36). The user of the site must be able to consistently locate buttons to navigate between the Web pages.

The navigation of a Web site can be either linear or nonlinear. Linear Web sites have little user choice; navigation requires the user to go step by step. Consider a user who is not able to review all of the information in one site visit. When he returns to the site, he may want to view what he has not yet seen. If the site is in a linear format, the user would still need to view pages 1, 2, and 3, because he could not jump to page 4. The use of paper and pencil for storyboarding often results in linear navigation.

A nonlinear format allows the user to have choice and access information on an as-needed basis. These sites are more complex for both the developer

Figure 6.3 Centered buttons.

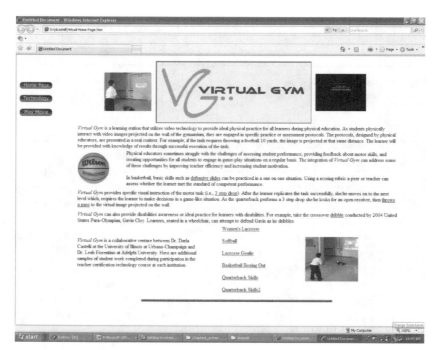

Figure 6.4 Vertical buttons in left column.

and the user and thus more difficult to create. The Inspiration software program promotes nonlinear designs.

The bottom line, whether the developer chooses a linear or nonlinear format, is that the design template should have a consistent look and feel and content should be organized in a systematic fashion, within a given theme. The easiest way to begin Web development is to select a template from the software package. The type of software selected will determine the nature of the templates. Often these templates are already predetermined by a school district or institution. The learning modules in this chapter provide details on how to access and use templates for Web development.

Insert Interactive Elements

The teacher must also determine the amount of interactivity desired. For example, will students simply view the Web site, or will they go to the site to link to other Web sites of interest? The amount of interactivity determines the degree of complexity and the number of pages to include in the Web site. For this reason, the degree of interactivity should be identified prior to beginning page design. (For example, during Women's and Girl's Sport History Month [February], a teacher may want to place a link to the KidsZone Women of Courage and Vision Web site [www.sportsline.com/u/kids/women/] on the page. This Web site uses Macromedia Flash to allow students to interact extensively with graphics.) Beginning Web developers should be careful about setting hyperlinks that may require advanced features. (See teacher modules 6.1 and 6.2 for details on how to create hyperlinks.)

Publish and Test the Web Page

Some Web developers suggest that a single Web page should be tested for a period of three to five years before additional pages are added to the Web site. Yet, if a teacher were to do so, the page would be obsolete before it reached the audience. We believe that pilot testing, peer review, and continual upgrading of materials will help to ensure the effectiveness and functionality of the Web site. Teachers should follow the steps outlined in this chapter and then upload their materials to the WWW, thus opening the door for feedback, modification, and revision.

During this phase it is critical that the teacher collaborate with the media or network specialist affiliated with the school or district. Web pages cannot be directly uploaded to the WWW without a password-protected file transfer protocol **(FTP)**. An FTP is how offline Web materials located on a local computer workstation are made available on the Internet. Most FTPs require the Web developer to log on with a password and then drag the Web folder from the desktop of the local computer workstation to the space on the server. Again, school districts often employ people to conduct this phase for teachers.

Finally, getting the Web site up and running is the most difficult part of development. This phase is referred to as publishing. Web pages often require an extended period of pilot testing before becoming completely functional. Teachers should select two or three peers to review the contents and functionality of the Web page before advertising its availability to students and parents. Web pages that contain spelling errors or are not functional on a variety of computers can embarrass teachers. Peers reviewing a site should also identify any potential bias or unintended opinions. Some school districts require that a committee review any materials prior to publication on the Internet. Teachers should be informed about the local policies before publishing Web sites that contain the name of the school or district.

SUMMARY

Chapter 5 addressed Web consumerism and the creation of Web Quests. Building on these skills, this chapter addressed the issue of Web pages and Web sites as a way for teachers to communicate with and disseminate information to students, parents, and the larger community. A seven-step approach to Web development was provided. Several precautions, such as copyright issues and protection of student identity, were embedded within the strategies. Teachers should collaborate with others within the school and seek assistance to acquire Web page templates, gain permission to upload to the WWW, and identify the school district policies for Web page evaluation. Many teachers already have Web sites, and some contain advanced interactive features. (To view a sample of effective physical education teacher Web sites, go to www.PElinks4u.com or www.pecentral.com.)

LEARNING MODULES

The learning modules are available to download from the companion Web site at www.HumanKinetics.com/PhysicalEducationTechnologyPlaybook.

The teacher modules in this chapter require teachers to use HTML editing software to create professional portfolios and their own Web sites.

The lesson plans in this chapter use the WWW as a means of promoting physical activity. Students need to be effective Web consumers and be able to access and share information found in a Web search.

Teacher Module 6.1 Web Pages as a Professional Portfolio

Teacher module 6.1 focuses on preservice teachers' development of a Web-based portfolio containing artifacts that offer evidence of professional growth. Using Mozilla Composer (free software downloadable from the Internet), teachers create five Web pages within a given theme. The content of these pages should meet the professional standards affiliated with future employment (e.g., teacher, coach, or personal trainer).

Teacher Module 06.1
Web Pages as a Professional Portfolio

Objective
To create at least five Web pages to be used as a professional portfolio that documents professional growth within a unique discipline of study.

National Standards for Beginning Physical Education Teachers
*Standard 5 Communication. Use knowledge of effective verbal, nonverbal, and media communication techniques to enhance learning and engagement in physical education settings.
*Standard 8 Reflection. Understand the importance of being a reflective practitioner and its contribution to overall professional development and actively seek opportunities to sustain professional growth.

Materials
*Computer workstations
*Internet connectivity
*Any HTML-editing software, such as Mozilla Composer, Adobe Dreamweaver, and Microsoft Office Suite (FrontPage, Publisher, Word, or PowerPoint)

Discussion Questions
*What do Web pages and professional growth have in common?
*What are examples of items that can serve as evidence of professional growth?

Directions
1. You will develop a Web site that includes evidence of reaching or exceeding National Standards for Professional Development. There are standards for physical education teachers, health education teachers, sport management and exercise science professionals, athletic coaches, and athletic trainers. You will search the World Wide Web (WWW) and locate the national standards that pertain to your specified professional certification.
2. You will create a Web site containing five linked page files (menu or main page, professional links page, resume page, photograph page, and professional standards page). The files should be organized using a template and contain a similar display and a professional portrait of the teacher on each page. Pages should be titled and saved as follows: (a) Main Menu (index.html), (b) Professional Links (prolinks.html), (c) Resume (resume.html), (d) Photos (photos.html), and (e) Professional Standards (standards.html). You are encouraged to create a theme that will be evident across the five files, while using good judgment about the content and graphics. A theme means consistently applying the same font, colors, and formatting across all of the five constructed Web pages.

Teacher Module 06.1 Web Pages as a Professional Portfolio   1
From *Physical Education Technology Playbook* by Darla Castelli and Leah Holland Fiorentino, 2008, Champaign, IL: Human Kinetics.

Teacher Module 6.1 Web Pages as a Professional Portfolio is available to download from the companion Web site.

Teacher Module 6.2 Web Development

The second teacher module requires teachers to use a Web development software program of their choice to communicate the policies, procedures, teacher expectations, and inclusiveness of a mock physical education program. This module is designed to help teachers refine their Web development skills, as well as reflect on the management issues related to physical education programming.

Teacher Module 06.2
Web Development

Objective
To create a Web site containing four pages that gives parents an overview of a mock physical education program.

National Standards for Beginning Physical Education Teachers
*Standard 3 Diverse Learners. Understand how individuals differ in their approaches to learning and create appropriate instruction adapted to these differences.
*Standard 5 Communication. Use knowledge of effective verbal, nonverbal, and media communication techniques to enhance learning and engagement in physical education settings.

Materials
*Computer workstations
*Internet connectivity

Accompanying File
TM06.2 Worksheet (Storyboard)

Discussion Questions
*What basic technology skills should every teacher have?
*What are some effective class activities (e.g., using Web sites) that give students more responsibility for their own learning?

Directions
In order to make some of the modules generally applicable to multiple contexts, in this module the teacher gets to select the software. The Web site must describe the class schedule, procedures, the curriculum, and programmatic attempts to meet the diverse student needs. A theme must be evident across the four pages, and developers should use good judgment in their choices of content and graphics.

1. Assemble a team of four or five people to work on the module.
2. Select HTML-editing software (i.e., Mozilla Composer, Microsoft FrontPage, or Adobe Dreamweaver) for the group to use to develop a Web site.
3. Determine the type of Web site to create.
4. Gather information and identify the important content for the Web pages.
5. Chunk the information by category.
6. Sketch a storyboard or concept map (filename: TM06.2 Worksheet).
7. Select a design template.
8. Insert interactive elements.
9. Save the Web page off-line for peer review by another work group.

Teacher Module 06.2 Web Development   1
From *Physical Education Technology Playbook* by Darla Castelli and Leah Holland Fiorentino, 2008, Champaign, IL: Human Kinetics.

Teacher Module 6.2 Web Development is available to download from the companion Web site.

Lesson Plan 6.1 Creating a New Game

In lesson plan 6.1, students are asked to search for information on the Internet and use it to design their own new games. Based on what they find, students create a new game to be played during physical education class. The students will try to incorporate elements found in video clips into the design of their new games.

Lesson Plan 06.1
Creating a New Game
Grades 6-8

Objective
To create new games that will be played during physical education class. An online program is used not only to create games but also to get tips from professional athletes.

National Standards for Physical Education
Standard 3: Participates regularly in physical activity.

Materials
*Computer workstations or laptops
*Internet connectivity

Accompanying Files
*LP06.1Student_Instructions
*LP06.1Worksheet (Your Game)

Set Induction
You and your classmates likely agree that teenagers need to move more to avoid the onset of childhood obesity–related ailments. But how can you get your friends up and moving? Maybe it has something to do with activities that are easily available. Are you tired of the same old games? Do some of your classmates avoid the same old games in physical education classes? Is there a way to make physical activity fun by creating new and challenging games and sports? What equipment would you use? What rules would you make? Would there be a winner and loser? Would it be a team activity or something that you and your friends could play as individuals?

Activity
1. Have the students access the Internet and go to:
   *http://kids.yahoo.com,
   *www.agameaday.com,
   *http://www.highlightskids.com, or
   *www.kidsrunning.com.
If you list these Web addresses in a text document, the students can follow the links by holding down the Ctrl key and selecting the link.
2. The students can take an ordinary game found online with no physical activity (e.g., word puzzles, inactive videogame, or educational game) and turn it into a physically active game. Students can also modify any sport into an activity that they would be interested in playing with their friends.
3. As the students are working on the computer, distribute copies of the worksheet, Your Game, so they can record their ideas.

Lesson Plan 06.1 Creating a New Game
From *Physical Education Technology Playbook* by Darla Castelli and Leah Holland Fiorentino, 2008, Champaign, IL: Human Kinetics.

Lesson Plan 6.1 Creating a New Game is available to download from the companion Web site.

Lesson Plan 6.2 Physical Activity in Your Town

The second lesson plan requires students to find information on the Internet related to physical activity options in the community. To make the assignment more authentic, students must create a Web page (using Microsoft Word) focused on how to encourage a friend to be more physically active.

Lesson Plan 06.2
Physical Activity in Your Town
Grades 6-8

Objective
To find information on the Internet about opportunities to be physically active in your area and generate a Web page that encourages a friend to participate in the activities.

National Standards for Physical Education
Standard 3: Participates regularly in physical activity.

Materials
*Computer workstations or laptops
*Internet connectivity

Accompanying File
LP06.2Student_Instructions

Set Induction
You have a friend who goes home every day after school and sits in front of the TV playing video games. You want to encourage him or her to be more physically active but do not know what you could do in your community. Are there online programs that promote physical activity among youth? Do the online programs have information about activities in your local area? Your task is to search the Internet for "things to do" and "places to play" in your area so that your friend can become more physically active.

Activity
1. Arrange your students across the computer stations or distribute Lesson Plan 06.2 Student Instructions: Physical Activity in Your Town to your students as a homework assignment. If you choose to give this as a homework assignment, remember to point out places in the community where students can gain free access to the Internet (e.g., public library, after school, and so on) because you want all students to have an equal opportunity to be successful with this task.
2. If this learning task is given as an in-class assignment, review with the students how to insert pictures and text into a Microsoft Word document.
3. Review how to add Web links to the Microsoft Word document.
4. Teach the students how to save the file as a Web page by going to *File*, then *Save As*. Have them type the file name in the section titled *Save as Type*. Remind the students to avoid long file names. Suggest that they use only eight characters. Once the title is entered, have the students use the drop-down list under *Save File As* to select *Web page*.
5. Have the students follow the steps outlined in Lesson Plan 06.2 Student Instructions: Physical Activity in Your Town to create their Web page.

Lesson Plan 06.2 Physical Activity in Your Town
From *Physical Education Technology Playbook* by Darla Castelli and Leah Holland Fiorentino, 2008, Champaign, IL: Human Kinetics.

Lesson Plan 6.2 Physical Activity in Your Town is available to download from the companion Web site.

Word Processing Enhancement Activities

Every sixth-grade student in your middle school is required to take a course called Intro to Desktop Publishing. As a steady stream of students flows into the locker room, you contemplate your own learning and junior high course work. You can't remember any courses that used technology. Suddenly you remember the typing course that you took during your senior year of high school. You reflect on the experiences of others in your family (you come from a long line of teachers, each with advanced degrees). The teaching professionals in your family all elected to become aficionados of different subject matters (physical education, language arts, and administration), yet you all share the bond of having participated in teacher preparation programs. When your father wrote his master's thesis, he used a typewriter. His thesis was 175 pages long, and he had to type each draft (he estimated six or seven) in its entirety. Today, you simply cut, paste, spell check, and grammar check, thus allowing the software to make many of the formatting decisions for you. Unlike your father, you have been through three home computers and have become quite savvy about Internet navigation, e-mail, and word processing. Yet your students have discovered features embedded in word processing software packages that were unknown to you. You head to the bookstore to read *Word Processing for Dummies* so you can bone up on what your sixth-graders already know and potentially use word processing for your own professional advancement.

The historical perspective provided in the preceding vignette reflects the experiences of some of us. Despite the fact that word processing (e.g., Microsoft Word, Corel Word Perfect) is one of the few software programs most teachers report being familiar with, many are not aware of the functions these programs offer. This chapter focuses on the advanced features of this technology that can help teachers enhance communication and establish collaborations. Word processing software offers a variety of templates, including those for constructing the following:

- Formal letters to parents and politicians
- Brochures for public relations efforts
- Newsletters to highlight positive aspects of programs
- Trifold flyers to advertise new initiatives
- Banners to get the attention of an audience
- Basic Web pages for WWW activities
- Labels to expedite tasks

Free templates are available online and are continually being expanded. Each template (prepared form) requires only that users type in key information, replacing the sample text with their own words. If the user has a current license for the software, then she is not required by copyright law to even change the text because she has purchased permission to use the template "as is." Word processing software can also provide word counts, the reading level of text, and grammatical feedback such as how many statements were made in the passive voice. These features, when working properly, increase teacher productivity by helping them develop professional products. Teachers should remember, however, that documents generated by these technologies are often the first impression presented to an administrator or a parent; therefore, they should be of the highest quality.

WORD PROCESSING FOR ADVOCACY

Advocacy is an important, undervalued responsibility of educators. Teacher advocates are those who speak on behalf of physical education programs. Specifically, materials generated with word processing software can be used to communicate with parents and link with community opportunities. A newsletter or brochure can serve as a medium for corresponding with parents. Some school districts have created trifold brochures describing their K-12 physical education curricula. The final page of such a document contains the specific physical education polices related to a single school in the district. Parents are required to sign the policy sheet indicating that they have read and reviewed the physical education policies with their child. This type of proactive communication has led to increased behavioral and policy compliance in physical education classes.

Word processing programs also enable people to create personal business cards. Teacher candidates who create their own business cards are sending a message to future employers that they are comfortable with technology and are capable of using advanced word processing features. A business card should be professional and project an image of a teacher who is affiliated with a quality program. Newsletters, brochures, and business cards are just a few items that can be created through word processing that allow teachers to present themselves professionally to parents and administrators.

WORD PROCESSING TO ENHANCE INSTRUCTION

Word processing can be used to create materials that enhance instruction. Teachers can design one-page fact sheets, study guides, and physical education newsletters to distribute to students. A one-page fact sheet contains a title, a brief summary or story, and a bulleted list of valuable information. Like a Microsoft PowerPoint presentation, each bullet should contain approximately seven words and be a phrase, not a sentence. Fact sheets can provide background information about a novel task (e.g., cradling in lacrosse, the biomechanical principles of force generation) or serve as a review of previously addressed content. Fact sheets should be brief to encourage students to read them, not drop them in the trash can.

The one-page fact sheet has been particularly effective for presenting health-related fitness content, such as statistics related to increases in physical inactivity among teens or increases in the number of overweight adolescents. A peer testimonial or tragic story can also be used to attract the attention of young readers. For example, a one-page fact sheet titled "Heart Attack at 10!" could recount the story of a 10-year-old boy who was overweight and inactive and had suffered what doctors believed to be a cardiac event. The teacher could paraphrase the story, provide a Web address of the full article, create a list of health statistics about teens, and then present possible solutions. The latter is the most important because scare tactics do not have a lasting impact. Fact sheets should be intended to start dialogues about the topic.

To help their physical education students progress toward the achievement of standard 2 (demonstrates understanding of movement concepts, principles, strategies, and tactics as they apply to the learning and performance of physical activities), teachers should provide students with the concepts and training principles related to the instructional unit. To hold students accountable for this terminology and content knowledge, many teachers use traditional assessment measures such as paper-and-pencil testing. A study guide would increase students' success rates as well as project a serious approach to learning. Study guides help students discriminate what information is of the utmost importance.

If exciting things are happening in the gym, a physical education newsletter is an ideal way to make others aware of them. For example, during sport education units, programs have used physical education newsletters to report how sport teams are performing in the culminating event. In a Sport Education unit, students assume various roles and responsibilities similar to those in real-life sport situations (e.g., referee, statistician, coach, player, media specialist). The media specialist can work with the game statistician to create a press release for the games or events that were conducted within physical education. Schools with radio and television services can broadcast video coverage or summary reports on tournament play. If no additional media services are available, this information can be placed in a simple newsletter.

SUMMARY

Many teachers report feeling comfortable with sending e-mail, searching the Internet, and using a word processor (National Center for Education Statistics, 2000). Although the percentage of teachers who use these technologies in the classroom has increased over a 10-year period from 21% to 43%, few use these technologies to enhance student learning. Ninety-nine percent of teachers report having computers in their classrooms or access to computers in their school buildings. Word processing software provided as part of the computer startup package could be used to advocate for student needs or program support. The bottom line is that teachers have word processing skills, but their skills are minimal, resulting in the underuse of this technology.

LEARNING MODULES

The learning modules are available to download from the companion Web site at www.HumanKinetics.com/PhysicalEducationTechnologyPlaybook.

Professional networking and the creation of student awards are the focuses of the teacher modules in this chapter. Teachers create their own business cards for distribution at professional meetings, conferences, and parent nights. The modules challenge teachers to go beyond their present word processing skills and create customized documents.

The lesson plans in this chapter focus on using word processing software to create a Web page and a physical activity calendar. The Web page development is designed for secondary physical education students, whereas the calendar targets elementary school students. The second lesson plan in this chapter requires students to purposefully plan their physical activity while away from formal physical education instruction. The module requires students to use a calendar template to plan one month of physical activity

Teacher Module 7.1 — Business Cards

Using Microsoft Word, teachers create and print customized business cards. These cards must include critical contact information such as e-mail address, street address, and phone numbers. The business card should reflect individuality through the inclusion of photos and promotional text. Teacher module 7.1 focuses on teachers' personality and professionalism.

Teacher Module 7.2 — Sport Education Awards

Teacher module 7.2 focuses on teachers' acknowledgments of student accomplishments through the creation of awards using word processing software. Many samples have been provided for both of the modules, because it is important to tailor the materials in these modules to the personality of the teacher and the context of the accomplishment.

Teacher Module 07.1
Business Cards

Objective
To create 10 professional business cards using Microsoft Word.

National Standards for Beginning Physical Education Teachers
Standard 9 Technology. Use information technology to enhance learning and personal and professional productivity.
Standard 10 Collaboration. Understand the necessity of fostering collaborative relationships with colleagues, parents/guardians, and community agencies to support the development of a physically educated person.

Materials
Computer workstations

Discussion Questions
*How should teachers present themselves when interviewing for a job?
*If you met someone on the street who could be a potential employer, how could you take advantage of this opportunity?

Directions
1. Open Microsoft Word.
2. Select *Tools* from the task bar.
3. Choose *Letters and Mailings.*
4. Select *Envelopes and Labels.*
5. Click the *Labels* tab.
6. Click *Options.*
7. Choose *8371 Business Card* in the *Product Number* sidebar (see figure 7.1).
8. Click *New Label* if the dimensions in the label information differ from the card size being used or to name each card design when multiple cards are constructed (see figure 7.2). Click *OK.*
9. Enter your personal information in the address box. This should include your title, name, address, phone numbers, e-mail address, and Web site address (see figure 7.3).
10. Click *New Document.* At this point you may add an image or change the font, color, or alignment to complete your project (remember to use a text box to add an image).

Assessment Criteria
1. Created a business card and printed a sheet of 10.
2. Included title, name, address, phone numbers, e-mail addresses, and Web site address on the business card.
3. Included at least one image on the card (images may be pictures, clipart, horizontal lines, or WordArt).
4. Created a professional business card.

Teacher Module 07.1 Business Cards   1
From *Physical Education Technology Playbook* by Darla Castelli and Leah Holland Fiorentino, 2008, Champaign, IL: Human Kinetics.

Teacher Module 7.1 Business Cards is available to download from the companion Web site.

Teacher Module 07.2
Sport Education Awards

Objective
To create at least three awards for your Sport Education unit's culminating event.

National Standards for Beginning Physical Education Teachers
Standard 4 Management and Motivation. Use and have an understanding of individual and group motivation and behavior to create a safe learning environment that encourages positive social interaction, active engagement in learning, and self-motivation.

Materials
Computer workstations

Accompanying Files
*TM_07.2_Worksheet1 (Badminton Champions)
*TM_07.2_Worksheet2 (Most Spirited)
*TM_07.2_Worksheet3 (Good Sporting Behavior Award)

Discussion Questions
*How can teachers acknowledge the efforts of students?
*How does this acknowledgment influence student motivation and engagement?

Directions
1. Determine the type, title, and number of student awards to give. Consider the following questions: Will everyone receive an award? Will students vote, or will the teacher select a winner? (If applicable, consult with your physical education colleagues to answer these questions in a consistent manner.)
2. Open Microsoft Word.
3. In a new document, change the document to landscape orientation by choosing *File,* then *Page Setup,* then *Landscape* under *Orientation* (see figure 7.1).
4. Choose a theme for your award by adjusting the page border; selecting a font color, style, and size; changing the size of the margins; or adding an image.
5. Use WordArt for creative text by clicking the WordArt icon.
6. Choose *Format* and then *Borders and Shading* to add a page border, background color, color around text, and so on (see figure 7.2).
7. Create at least three different awards. See worksheets 1, 2, and 3 for examples of awards.

Assessment Criteria
1. Printed at least three awards.
2. Used appropriate content.
3. Included at least one image on each award.
4. Created unique and creative awards.

Teacher Module 07.2 Sport Education Awards   1
From *Physical Education Technology Playbook* by Darla Castelli and Leah Holland Fiorentino, 2008, Champaign, IL: Human Kinetics.

Teacher Module 7.2 Sport Education Awards is available to download from the companion Web site.

Lesson Plan 7.1 Microsoft Word Web Pages

Microsoft Word Web Pages introduces students to the world of Web development through the use of word processing software. Although Web development features are limited in word processing software, students can create fully functional Web pages displaying what they have learned during physical education. The topic must be preapproved by the physical education teacher and meet the assessment criteria.

Lesson Plan 07.1
Microsoft Word Web Pages
Grades 8-12

Objective
To use Microsoft Word to design and create a Web page to display what you learned during physical education.

National Standards for Physical Education
*Standard 2: Demonstrates understanding of movement concepts, principles, strategies, and tactics as they apply to the learning and performance of physical activities.
*Standard 6: Values physical activity for health, enjoyment, challenge, self-expression, and/or social interaction.

Materials
*Computer workstations
*Internet connectivity

Accompanying File
LP07.1Student_Instructions

Set Induction
Have you ever wondered how Web sites are created? Did you know that you could create your own Web site using Microsoft Word? Today you will get to experiment and make your own!

Activity
1. Before developing Web pages, students need to identify the information or idea they wish to share (e.g., the history of a sport, how to get started if one were interested in playing a specific sport, or how science and physical education are interrelated). You can assign topics, or students can select them individually or in small groups. At the very least, we suggest that you develop a list of acceptable topics and allow students to make informed choices from the list. In addition, the students must identify the target audience that will view their Web pages, because that will affect its content. A target audience might be other physical education students, elementary students, or seniors within the community.
2. Once they have chosen their topics and identified their audiences, students should investigate other Web pages on the Internet that could provide them with information. Help them collect information in ways that do not result in plagiarism. Remind students that information taken from Web sites must be referenced as well as rephrased.
3. Finally, the students should collect graphic images from Web sites, scan images that they have found in print, capture still images using digital cameras, or use clipart galleries to enhance their Web pages. Using images from Web sites for educational purposes is permissible if a citation is provided and if the presentation is spontaneous and educational. Keeping student Web pages and using the images repeatedly would be a copyright violation.

Lesson Plan 07.1 Microsoft Word Web Pages
From *Physical Education Technology Playbook* by Darla Castelli and Leah Holland Fiorentino, 2008, Champaign, IL: Human Kinetics.

Lesson Plan 7.1 Microsoft Word Web Pages is available to download from the companion Web site.

Lesson Plan 7.2 Activity Calendar

This lesson plan has students create one-month physical activity plans for the entire family, because the involvement of family members supports regular engagement in physical activity. Adhering to physical activity guidelines, students identify activities for at least five days per week that last at least 60 minutes (Corbin, Pangrazi & Le Masurier, 2004; National Association for Sport and Physical Education, 2004).

Lesson Plan 07.2
Activity Calendar
Grades 4-5

Objective
To create an activity calendar to help your family and friends be more active.

National Standards for Physical Education
Standard 6: Values physical activity for health, enjoyment, challenge, self-expression, and/or social interaction.

Materials
*Computer workstations
*Internet connectivity
*Printer

Accompanying Files
*LP07.2Student_Instructions
*LP07.2Worksheet (Sample April 2017 Calendar)

Set Induction
You want to help your family and friends be more physically active. You decide to organize activities on a calendar so everyone knows when and where each event is and how long it will be. This way, there will be no excuse for not participating in the activity!

Activity
1. The students will be using word processing software to create a physical activity calendar. We suggest Microsoft Word; however, another word processor with calendar templates will do just fine. You can have the students complete this lesson during physical education class or in a computer lab, or you can give it to the students as a homework assignment.
2. Working individually or in pairs, have the students open the software and a calendar template.
3. You may want to have the students complete a physical activity calendar for the current month or for an extended vacation period. It is up to you.
4. The students will be asking you where to save their calendar. You could have them save it to the desktop of their computers, a shared folder on the intranet, or a flash drive. What works best depends on your computer lab setup. If you are not sure what to do, consult your technical support staff.
5. As the students are working on their calendars, encourage them to be physically active for at least 60 minutes on most days of the week. The student instructions recommend being active at least five days per week.

Lesson Plan 07.2 Activity Calendar
From *Physical Education Technology Playbook* by Darla Castelli and Leah Holland Fiorentino, 2008, Champaign, IL: Human Kinetics.

Lesson Plan 7.2 Activity Calendar is available to download from the companion Web site.

Desktop Publishing: Brochures and Banners

As part of the school wellness team, you have planned a day of physical activity for your school. You have invited parents, community members, and representatives of wellness resources within your community to participate in physical activity (teachers, parents, and students alike) simultaneously. The planning took months, but with the help of a few parents, you were able to organize this day. Your Wellness Day concept is welcomed by the administration as a viable outcome of your newly enacted school wellness plan. As one administrator stated, "Childhood obesity is a real issue that schools are going to have to deal with, whether they like it or not. A comprehensive approach involving parents has the most potential to be successful. In general, increased parental involvement as well as physical fitness is related to academic achievement in schools." With a limited budget, you were able to make this happen because of the materials you generated with your desktop publishing skills.

Recent application of the ecological systems theory (EST) to physical education programming has led to the resurgence of the idea that physical education teachers are responsible for extending the curriculum beyond the school and into the community. This is because the home environment and larger community are especially influential on youth physical activity (Sallis, Prochaska & Taylor, 2000). More specifically, within the home environment, parental overweight status, diet, access to facilities, and time spent outdoors have strong associations with the amount of physical activity children engage in. Reports also note that access to and participation in community sport programs, sibling attitudes toward and participation in physical activity, and overall opportunities to exercise are influential in the choices adolescents make regarding personal activity levels. To address some of the current needs of students, this chapter relates to NASPE teaching standards 5 (communication), 9 (technology), and 10 (collaboration) by addressing desktop publishing software and the creation of public relations materials.

The EST first idealized by Bronfenbrenner (1977) uses a multilevel model to illustrate the levels and interaction of environmental factors that may influence human behavior. Sallis and Owen's 1997 adaptation of this model to youth physical activity resulted in physical education teachers rethinking how they promote physical activity and address the physical activity needs of youth. The behavior of an individual, which can be defined as a lifestyle, is influenced by multiple factors beyond those found in the physical education program. It is shortsighted to think that youth physical activity stems explicitly from physical education.

However, given the present mind-set, a physical education teacher must develop a means of promoting physical activity across the entire school day and beyond, requiring the establishment of strong community relations. One of the most effective ways for a teacher to promote physical activity within the school day is to become involved in the design of the school wellness plan, which was required for all schools in the United States by the 2006-2007 academic year (House Education and Workforce Committee, 2004). The U.S. Congress recognized that schools play a critical role in promoting optimal student health, preventing childhood obesity, and combating problems associated with poor nutrition and physical inactivity. This is more than just a health issue; healthy nutritional choices and increased physical activity levels increase the chances for children to be academically successful.

All agencies that participate in the U.S. National School Lunch, Breakfast, or Milk Programs were required to establish a local wellness policy by the beginning of school year 2006-2007 (House Education and Workforce Committee, 2004). The legislation placed the responsibility of developing a wellness policy at the local level, so that the individual needs of each district could be addressed. Teams were to be formed to develop local policies. Membership on these teams would give physical education teachers a say in the daily physical activity opportunities for the students within the school site. As a result of the instituted wellness policies, some schools reported that they reinstated active recess, extended physical education instructional time, and enacted physical activity–specific before- and after-school programs.

Another way that physical education teachers can promote physical activity throughout and beyond the school day is to promote community involvement. As mentioned earlier, the home environment and immediate community play vital roles in the physical activity levels of youth. It has therefore become imperative that physical education teachers find a way to develop and enact explicit partnerships with various community resources.

Technology can play an important role in facilitating the physical education teacher's position on the school wellness team and in community partnerships. Specifically, desktop publishing is a means of creating promotional materials and public relations initiatives. As part of the Microsoft Office suite, teachers can use Microsoft Publisher to create banners, brochures, flyers, or one-page fact sheets.

MICROSOFT PUBLISHER

Computer software such as Microsoft Publisher helps users format text, organize numerical data, and create materials that display visual graphics. Depending on the desired product (e.g., banners, brochures, one-page fact sheets) and the intent of the materials (e.g., publicize a Wellness Day, inform parents about the benefits of physical activity, or announce events related to the curriculum), desktop publishing software can organize text and graphics into appealing advertisements. Materials produced by desktop publishers include books, business cards, calendars, magazines, newsletters and newspapers, packaging, slides, and tickets. However, the focus of this chapter is the creation of brochures and banners. Desktop publishing software allows users to create professional products without incurring professional costs.

Advances in desktop publishing software and printer capabilities have enhanced the quality of materials and expanded the capabilities of amateur desktop publishers. The Internet has assisted novice publishers in the refinement of their skills because many additional features are available through freeware. For example, free clipart, photos, and fonts can be found on the World Wide Web (WWW). An additional advantage for novice users is the sequential steps offered by the software wizard, thus providing a built-in proofing system. By using the keyboard and a mouse, users can make decisions about fonts, spacing, displays, and graphic illustrations related to the promotional materials; however, users must start with the end in mind.

The initial screen in Microsoft Publisher (figure 8.1) requires users to select the type of product they wish to generate and the form in which they want the product generated: publications for print, Web sites and e-mail, design sites, blank publications. This first step enables the software to make decisions regarding the quality and size of the graphics. For example, if a picture is of a very high quality,

Figure 8.1 Getting started with Microsoft Publisher.

it will load slowly on the WWW and may not even load at all on some computers using dial-up modems. Users who select *Publications for Print* are given a choice of templates that are organized by the type of output (e.g., banners, brochures; see figure 8.2).

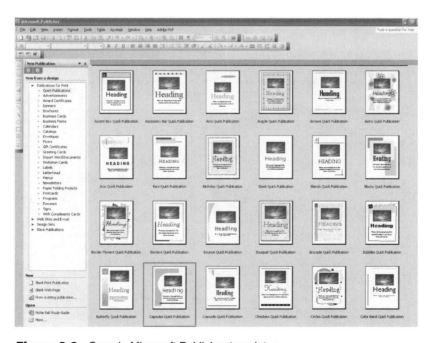

Figure 8.2 Sample Microsoft Publisher templates.

The category of *Quick Publications* offers several one-page templates that have a single picture and text in a large font. These templates are in specific color schemes, whereas another category, *Advertisements,* is exclusively created for black-and-white displays. Users without access to color printers may elect to create the promotional materials from the *Advertisements* category.

Brochures

The *Brochures* category offers templates for creating trifold brochures that can display a large amount of information (see figure 8.3). The intent of these brochures is to introduce many information sources at once, not just a single idea, as in a one-page fact sheet or brochures created in the *Quick Publications* category. Trifold brochures set out to grab readers' attention, hold their interest, and move them to action.

Trifold brochures are ideal for physical education teachers who want to introduce program policies and procedures to students and parents. The front page of the brochure should catch the attention of the reader through a combination of graphics and text placed into headers. The school name and logo should be graphically displayed, and the physical education program or specific curriculum title should be in bold text. To hold the attention of the reader, the brochure should contain a brief narrative about the mission or goals of the physical education program. Teacher expectations should be listed in a bulleted format for quick review by students or parents. Specific policies and procedures should also be in a list format and included on the inside of the brochure. The policies should be phrased in positive but firm statements, such as, "Remember that proper footwear is required for participation in physical education classes," as opposed to, "No street shoes on the gymnasium floor."

The final part of a brochure should require action from the reader. For example, the back page could require a signature from parents that they have reviewed and understand the program's policies and procedures. It could also suggest that parents discuss these policies with their children. This action requires the reader to acknowledge the program's policies and procedures and commit to working within the structure. This is just one example of a brochure used by school districts to communicate with parents and attempt to increase parental involvement in the schools.

Brochures can also be created by students as a physical education homework assignment. An example would be for students to identify possible physical activity opportunities within the community. They could then work in small groups to create brochures for community programs. This project would require students to gather information about the program and then display it in a way that catches the attention of adolescent readers, holds their attention, and provides an opportunity for action (e.g., including contact information). The lesson plans for this chapter require students to create brochures that advertise local health clubs or promote new games created by the group members.

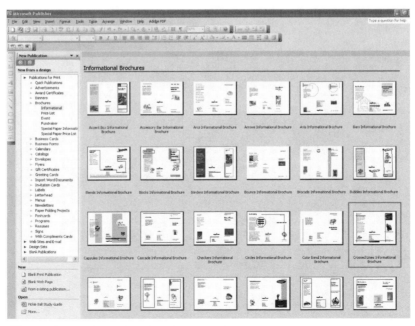

Figure 8.3 Informational brochure templates.

Banners

When users select a banner template, they are provided with at least nine options for a banner style (see figure 8.4), most of which fall into personal celebratory categories such as holiday events. Perhaps the banner used most frequently in physical education is the Team Spirit banner. Once the user has selected the category, he is prompted to input contact information to be included on the banner.

If the banner requires action from the reader, then the inclusion of personal contact information is an important and valuable step (see figure 8.5). However, if the information is deemed unnecessary, the user can skip this step and simply close the window.

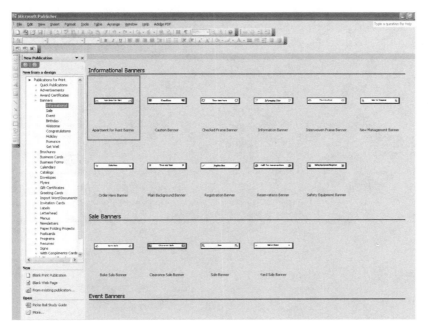

Figure 8.4 Informational banner templates.

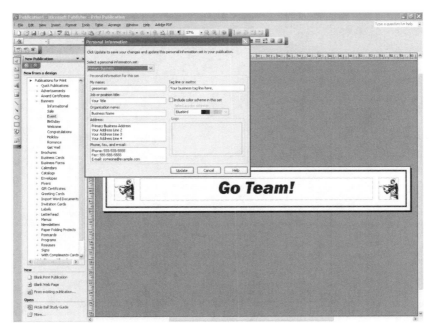

Figure 8.5 Adding personal information.

The user must then select the size of the banner (e.g., 5, 6, 8, or 10 feet), the color scheme, and the font scheme. By clicking on the picture that is already embedded in the banner template, the user can alter the picture or import an image from clipart or a file. After importing the picture, the user must type in the desired text and modify the font size and type. The text on banners should be like a title, brief and to the point. Banners are used to get attention and then encourage the reader to ask more questions.

Banners can be used to promote all-day events such as the Wellness Day described in the opening vignette or simply be used within the physical education facility to promote team spirit or a Sport Education culminating event (Siedentop, Hastie & van der Mars, 2005). For example, a Sport Education instructional season of basketball that requires role playing and sport-specific responsibilities (e.g., players, coaches, referees, statisticians, publicists) could use a banner to identify each team name. As part of the Sport Education culminating event, March Madness, teams could also use banners to track the points they have accumulated for good sporting behavior, wins, team spirit, or media reports. The lesson plans for this chapter require the use of desktop publishing software to produce promotional materials for alternative curricular events such as those engendered by participation in a Sport Education season.

SUMMARY

Physical education teachers are responsible for the promotion and practice of physical activity throughout the school day and beyond. Though still considered novel, the idea of the physical education teacher as physical activity director is catching on rapidly throughout the United States, as childhood obesity receives attention in the media. Technology such as desktop publishing can help teachers promote physical activity. Desktop publishing facilitates the creation of flyers, banners, brochures, and posters and can provide a means for communication and collaboration. The software is user-friendly and laden with entertaining templates for immediate use.

LEARNING MODULES

The learning modules are available to download from the companion Web site at www.HumanKinetics.com/PhysicalEducationTechnologyPlaybook.

The teacher learning modules for this chapter require teachers to use Microsoft Word and Microsoft Publisher to inform both parents and students of the program's policies and procedures. Many believe that such communications help establish routine appropriate behaviors on the part of students.

This chapter contains two lesson plans. Students are responsible for creating a curriculum-related banner and a trifold brochure describing the ideal health club facility. It is important for students to understand that there are a variety of ways to appreciate and be engaged in sport activities. These lesson plans encourage adolescents to take responsibility for their own physical activity. Basic skills are important to practice during the school years, because students need to begin the transfer of knowledge of health-related fitness to their lives beyond school.

Teacher Module 8.1   Public Relations

The first teacher module involves creating one-page fact sheets related to the current public health issue of childhood obesity. Using Microsoft Word, teachers select a template and add text and a picture to the fact page.

Teacher Module 8.2   Parent Night Information

The second teacher module results in the production of a trifold brochure, generated with a Microsoft Publisher template. This module requires teachers to consider the policies and procedures related to their programs. Specifically, teachers must consider what content will capture parents' attention during an information night, how to hold their attention, and what action the parents should take. The brochure should include the program's policies and procedures, grading criteria, the teacher's personal philosophy, semester and yearly activities, and ways parents can become involved with physical activities at the school. Teacher contact information and emergency contact information should also be included.

Teacher Module 08.1
Public Relations

Objective
To develop a one-page promotional brochure directed at the public health issue of childhood obesity. The brochure should encourage physical activity within and beyond the school setting.

National Standards for Beginning Physical Education Teachers
Standard 9 Technology. Use information technology to enhance learning and personal and professional productivity.

Materials
*Computer workstations
*Color printer

Discussion Questions
*How can teachers communicate with students' parents and the community?
*How can teachers share important health-related issues beyond the classroom or gymnasium?
*Is a comprehensive approach to school wellness possible without the support of parents and the local community?

Directions
1. Open Microsoft Word. From the *File* menu, select *New*, then *Templates on Office Online*.
2. From the templates page, select *Business and Legal*, then *Marketing*, then *Brochures and Booklets* (see figure 8.1). You will have several brochure styles to choose from; be sure to preview all of the styles before making a final choice.
3. For this specific task, be sure to select a style that has a Microsoft Word version.
4. Select the option *Download It Now*. When the download is complete, a file will open up in Microsoft Word.
5. Because the brochure has been set in a template format, text boxes have been set to maximize space usage. Follow the template format to maintain the constraints on the pages. To customize the template within the constraints, use the *Insert* key, which will then overwrite the text that is already in the text box.
6. Be original and creative with respect to the topic of childhood obesity issues and strategies to decrease the occurrence in your local community.
7. Include two inserted images that add power to your message. (Inserted images must be within a text box to maintain the page constraints in the template.)
8. Save your work and print a copy of your brochure.

Assessment Criteria
1. Created a one-page brochure with text and graphics directed at the public health issue of childhood obesity.
2. Used proper grammar, usage, and mechanics.

Teacher Module 08.1 Public Relations
From *Physical Education Technology Playbook* by Darla Castelli and Leah Holland Fiorentino, 2008, Champaign, IL: Human Kinetics.

Teacher Module 8.1   Public Relations is available to download from the companion Web site.

Teacher Module 08.2
Parent Night Information

Objective
To create a trifold brochure to inform parents of the policies and procedures of your physical education program.

National Standards for Beginning Physical Education Teachers
Standard 5 Communication. Use knowledge of effective verbal, nonverbal, and media communication techniques to enhance learning and engagement in physical education settings.
Standard 10 Collaboration. Understand the necessity of fostering collaborative relationship with colleagues, parents/guardians, and community agencies to support the development of a physically educated person.

Materials
*Computer workstations
*Color printer
*Microsoft Publisher

Discussion Questions
*What are the expectations for students in your physical education program?
*What does a prepared student look like?
*What is the best method to proactively encourage students to be prepared for your class?

Directions
1. Open Microsoft Publisher.
2. From the *File* menu, select *New*, then *Publications for Print*, then *Brochures*.
3. From the template page, select an informational brochures template. This will launch the personal information wizard, which prompts you to type in your personal contact information.
4. Enter your contact information in the spaces provided. When completed, click *OK*.
5. In the left-hand column, make choices regarding the format of the brochure, selecting the page size, customer address, and form.
6. Select *File*, then *Save* to preserve a copy of the template file.
7. By selecting various areas on the brochure, you can add your own text and insert pictures. Select *Insert*, then *Pictures*, then either *From Clipart* or *From a File*. As in Microsoft Word, inserted images must be within a text box.
8. Because the brochure has been set in a template format, text boxes have been set to maximize space usage. You will want to maintain the constraints on the pages. To customize the template within the constraints, use the *Insert* key to overwrite the text that is already in the text box.
9. The brochure should include the program's policies and procedures, grading criteria, your personal teaching philosophy, planned semester and yearly activities, and ways that parents can become involved with physical activities at the school. Your contact information and emergency contact information should also be included in the appropriate space.

Teacher Module 08.2 Parent Night Information
From *Physical Education Technology Playbook* by Darla Castelli and Leah Holland Fiorentino, 2008, Champaign, IL: Human Kinetics.

Teacher Module 8.2   Parent Night Information is available to download from the companion Web site.

Lesson Plan 08.1
Banner for a Sport Education Season
Grades 9-12

Objective
To develop a banner using Microsoft Publisher that displays your sport education team's colors, name, sport, record, good sporting behavior recognition, or teamwork accomplishments. This banner will help to promote enthusiasm for the culminating event (e.g., track meet or soccer tournament) as well as the affiliation and spirit of your team. It must also contain at least one image and be printed for display.

National Standards for Physical Education
*Standard 5: Exhibits responsible personal and social behavior that respects self and others in physical activity settings.
*Standard 6: Values physical activity for health, enjoyment, challenge, self-expression, and/or social interaction.

Materials
*Computer workstations
*Color and banner printer
*Microsoft Publisher

Accompanying File
LP08.1Student_Instructions

Set Induction
As the publicist for your sport education team, write a list of all the ways you could promote the culminating sport education event in your school (e.g., morning announcements, banners, and so on). What are the advantages and disadvantages of the items on your list? Why would a banner be a good first task?

Activity
During a unit that used a sport education alternative curriculum model (for more details, see Siedentop, Hastie, and van de Mars, 2004), students participate in authentic sport seasons in which they take on many different roles. For example, during March Madness, you have set up a basketball sport education unit. You have student teams, and within those teams, you have assigned specific roles (e.g., coach, player, referee, media specialist, and so on) for each student. This activity is designed for the media specialist or a select few students to create a team banner. As suggested by Siedentop et al. (2004), the more authentic and spirited the experience, the higher the student engagement; therefore, the creation of banners will help to foster team spirit and affiliation.

Lesson Plan 08.1 Banner for a Sport Education Season   1
From *Physical Education Technology Playbook* by Darla Castelli and Leah Holland Fiorentino, 2008, Champaign, IL: Human Kinetics.

Lesson Plan 8.1   Banner for a Sport Education Season is available to download from the companion Web site.

Lesson Plan 08.2
Redesigning Recreation
Grades 9-12

Objective
To promote physical activity in adolescents by creating a trifold brochure containing the important information about the sport and recreation opportunities available in the local community.

National Standards for Physical Education
Standard 6: Values physical activity for health, enjoyment, challenge, self-expression, and/or social interaction.

Materials
*Computer workstations
*Color printer
*Internet connectivity

Accompanying File
LP08.2Student_Instructions

Set Induction
What can we do in our community to be physically active? Where can we go? Are there resources in the community that could be redesigned to meet the physical activity interests and needs of adolescents? How much would it cost to make changes to an already established community resource? Whom can you contact about making this idea a reality?

Activity
1. Lead a class discussion about all of the ways in which the students are physically active in the community. Focus your attention on physical activities that are unrelated to the school (e.g., karate clubs, golf courses, skate parks, ski or hiking trails, horseback riding, archery, and so on).
2. Once the class has generated a list of opportunities within the community, explain that each student will create a trifold brochure about an activity, outside of school athletics and clubs, that they are currently do. If they are not active, they may either work with an active friend or research opportunities in the community (see Lesson Plan 06.2 Student Instructions: Physical Activity in Your Town).
3. Each student should select a physical activity opportunity to share. You may want to ask them what they have selected before they get too far. Have them use the Internet to retrieve the contact information about their topics.
4. Using Microsoft Publisher or any other desktop publishing software, the students should begin crafting their brochure by typing the information into the template.
5. The students may add clipart or pictures to enhance their brochure.

Lesson Plan 08.2 Redesigning Recreation   1
From *Physical Education Technology Playbook* by Darla Castelli and Leah Holland Fiorentino, 2008, Champaign, IL: Human Kinetics.

Lesson Plan 8.2   Redesigning Recreation is available to download from the companion Web site.

Lesson Plan 8.1   Banner for a Sport Education Season

The first lesson requires students to use Microsoft Publisher to create banners as sport publicists in a sport education season. Publicists must brainstorm ways to promote the culminating event of the sport education season and then create a team banner, spirit banner, or a banner scoreboard to track team progress.

Lesson Plan 8.2   Redesigning Recreation

Using Microsoft Publisher, students generate trifold brochures to be used to promote extending physical activity beyond the school day. This lesson puts students in a position to advocate for the resources that interest them (e.g., skate parks, swimming pools, health clubs). Students identify community resources and design brochures that introduce their ideas regarding facility usage to encourage adolescent participation.

Newsletters

At the beginning of the school year, you started a walking club that used pedometers to promote more active recess sessions and to monitor students' progress toward their physical activity goals. The students were excited about the program and many signed up, but you did not have enough pedometers for everyone who wanted to participate. You were also lacking incentives to maintain the enthusiasm that came with the start of a new school year and program. You decided that you had enough news to create and distribute your own *PE Milers' Club* newsletter. This one-page flyer was intended to inform parents about the health choices children were making during the school day. Additionally, you hoped to get enough pedometers for everyone to be able to participate.

After distributing the newsletter, you not only received what you needed for incentives but also heard from families that their children had increased their recorded steps after school and on the weekends. The program then expanded to a family initiative in which students could receive beads and wristbands whenever they were physically active on the weekend with or without their family members. As a result of this increase in interest in the program, you needed to acquire additional pedometers and sent letters to several local businesses seeking support for the initiative.

Similar to other chapters, this one attempts to enhance communication (e.g., teacher to parents, teacher to student, student to community) and establish collaborations, particularly with community members. Content in this chapter also focuses on student management and motivation through the use of newsletters.

Newsletters are easy to create and have high advocacy potential. Unlike classroom teachers or teachers in other specializations, physical education teachers usually come in contact with every student in the school. Communicating with every student, and their parents, particularly in a large school, can be a daunting task. A monthly or quarterly newsletter can effectively deliver valuable information in a timely manner to both students and parents.

As a result of state and federal legislation in the United States, schools are under tremendous pressure to improve students' academic performance. As a result, some schools require students to participate in academic remediation programs in place of physical education classes, some have reduced physical education class time, and others have eliminated physical education teacher positions in lieu of academic classroom teacher positions. At this time, the state of Illinois remains the only state to mandate daily K-12 physical education; however, given the present pressure on schools to improve academic performance or lose vital funding, many schools in Illinois have applied for waivers so students can spend more time in language arts, mathematics, and science classes. Although the creation of a newsletter may not directly save the job of a physical education teacher, it does increase exposure of the program to the larger community and may increase the support of key players.

INITIAL NEWSLETTER CONSIDERATIONS

Before developing and disseminating a newsletter, a teacher must decide on the name, who will contribute, and the layout format. A brief, clever title can capture attention and entice people to read the newsletter. Using a name contest to kick off the initial newsletter would create a form of free advertising at the school as well as within the larger community. The teacher could offer a prize for naming the newsletter and identify the winner(s) during the morning school announcements. Encouraging

students to name the newsletter connects them to the effort and provides a feeling of ownership, which may motivate them to participate in the activities reported in the newsletter.

Mentioning specific students' physical activity achievements in a newsletter can give students the incentive to participate in physical activities while also advocating for the physical education program. Before printing students' names in the newsletter, however, teachers should receive written approval from the school administration. Normally, administrators who have approved of the creation and dissemination of a school newsletter will endorse the highlighting of student efforts. School administrators should also receive final draft copies of the newsletter prior to duplication and distribution to ensure that all information is accurate and that the document adheres to all school district policies. Because each school district has unique policies regarding the public use of students' names, teachers should be aware of and strictly adhere to district policies. A request for written approval from the administrator will serve as official documentation of compliance as well as evidence of teacher initiative.

Another way to pique students' interest in a newsletter is to add student artwork. Doing so also helps families connect with the newsletter content and become further invested in the effort. Physical education teachers can encourage elementary students to create artwork as physical education homework by asking them, for example, to draw a picture of what they did in physical education today. Physical education teachers can also work in concert with art educators in a variety of visual media areas. To further the interdisciplinary connections, classroom teachers can ask elementary students to write captions for their drawings. Classroom teachers might also be enlisted to assign students the task of writing letters to their parents encouraging them to be physically active to help prevent future health problems.

CREATING A TEMPLATE

The physical education teacher should create a consistent look for the newsletter, especially at the elementary school level where students bring home tons of paper for parents to weed through. The newsletter should display a healthy, positive image and possibly use school colors for the paper or the ink (note, however, that dark backgrounds sometimes cause eye strain, and it may be difficult to print in a white or light-colored ink). In general, a bright-colored paper and dark ink are recommended. Teachers who are struggling to get started can consider using Microsoft Word templates, which can be downloaded from the Internet and modified.

NEWSLETTER CONTENT

Regardless of the template and design selected for the newsletter, the teacher must use proper English (grammar, usage, and mechanics) in the text of the newsletter. The use of slang or derogatory terms will have adverse effects on the teacher and the program, which is contrary to the intent of the newsletter. The teacher should be aware of the "hidden curriculum"; that is, subtle messages embedded within the newsletter. For example, do girls appear as often as boys in photos? Does the newsletter acknowledge the efforts of all students regardless of physical ability? Is the newsletter reflective of the cultural diversity of the school? Sensitivity to these issues and cultural responsiveness are necessary characteristics of the physical educator who is now a publisher.

An additional consideration is the reading level of the target audience. Most word processing software programs allow users to check the reading level of a document. For example, in Microsoft Word, the user can select *Tools, Options,* and *Spelling and Grammar,* and then check *Show readability statistics* to receive a report of the Flesch reading ease as well as the Flesch-Kincaid grade level each time the document is spell-checked. This way the physical educator can produce text that is at an appropriate reading level for the target audience.

DISTRIBUTION

Although the cost of distribution should be incurred by school districts, teachers should be both cost conscious and consistent. They should consider how much information to include in each issue, who is going to contribute to the writing, and how much time is available to work on the newsletter before even deciding how often to generate the newsletter. Interdisciplinary approaches have been helpful with these considerations; for example, gifted or enrichment programs can be enlisted to help. Teachers who offer these programs are often looking for creative and challenging projects for their students. Classroom teachers can invite students in special programs to contribute articles for the physical education newsletter, or they can assign certain students to act as classroom reporters and write brief statements about the activities the class shared during the current week's physical education classes.

Having decided who is going to contribute, the teacher must determine how often the newsletter should be distributed to parents or other pertinent individuals. A weekly newsletter may lose its effect in a short time, but a quarterly or monthly newsletter should be able to maintain an impact throughout the academic year. The physical educator may also want to time the release of the newsletter to correspond with key events in the school, such as report cards or parent–teacher conferences.

ONLINE OR HARD COPY?

The majority of physical educators elect to have a hard copy newsletter as the initial format; however, increasing numbers of physical educators choose to have electronic newsletters. Online formats are more organic and dynamic than a hard copy version because of the ease of updates and distribution access. An electronic newsletter can go directly to a family's e-mail address rather than home through "backpack delivery," placing physical education news into the mainstream of family conversations. Information can be updated easily and rapidly circulated among parents as well as school personnel. Of course, because some community members may not have access to online services, hard copy newsletters should always be available. A final consideration prior to planning an online version of the newsletter is the technology skills required to load files onto an Internet site. (For additional information, see chapter 6.)

The creation of online newsletters requires advanced Web development as well as telecommunication skills. Teachers must be able to generate the newsletter in HTML and distribute it via e-mail or upload it to the school district server. These newsletters will need to be updated continually if the purpose is to have individuals access them on a regular basis, as readers will become disenchanted if they continue to check for an updated newsletter and only see old information. The newsletter that arrives via e-mail should be sent on a quarterly basis only so as not to invade people's privacy. The best mechanism for distributing online newsletters is to request that families subscribe and then set the distribution list for those names only.

UNANTICIPATED BENEFITS

Newsletters (hard copy or online) that go home on a regular basis can have unanticipated benefits. For example, perhaps a student's mother works for the newspaper and reads all of the wonderful things that are happening during physical education classes. She might go to the editor of the newspaper and suggest a story on how this one program is attempting to address the issue of childhood obesity. Another example might be a local bank that has small grants available for programs that address youth health. A parent who is a member of the bank's grant-funding team might read the newsletter and contact the physical educator to

suggest that he apply for the grant because his program is exactly the type of project the bank would like to fund.

SUMMARY

Newsletters are a viable and cost effective means of disseminating advocacy information to a larger audience. Student involvement is an important factor contributing to the ultimate success of the newsletter. The teacher must determine the name, type, format, and design template of the newsletter and continually upgrade the newsletter materials. The term *news* implies recent, not past, events so currency of information is critical to the impact of the newsletter. The teacher must determine what content is valuable enough to distribute to parents. Student photos, artwork, and classwork can be included, with parental permission as mentioned in chapter 6.

LEARNING MODULES

The learning modules are available to download from the companion Web site at www.HumanKinetics.com/PhysicalEducationTechnologyPlaybook.

Teacher Module 9.1   Program Newsletter

The first teacher module requires teachers to display original work related to their ideal physical education program, using Microsoft Office suite. Teachers must create attractive names for their newsletters. They may choose topics such as Jump Rope for Heart Month or the Physical Education Winter Olympics.

> **Teacher Module 09.1**
> **Program Newsletter**
>
> **Objective**
> To create a newsletter containing the latest events from the school's physical education program that can be distributed to students and parents.
>
> **National Standards for Beginning Physical Education Teachers**
> *Standard 4 Management and Motivation. Use and have an understanding of individual and group motivation and behavior to create a safe learning environment that encourages positive social interaction, active engagement in learning, and self-motivation.
> *Standard 5 Communication. Use knowledge of effective verbal, nonverbal, and media communication techniques to enhance learning and engagement in physical education settings.
>
> **Materials**
> *Computer workstations
> *Printer
> *Internet connectivity
>
> **Discussion Questions**
> *In what ways can teachers communicate information about the latest events from the physical education program to the larger community?
> *What are key features of this communication?
> *How can teachers be sure that all members of the community can have access to this communication?
>
> **Guidelines**
> *The newsletter should identify your philosophy, goals and objectives, standards, and expectations for the program. The content of your newsletter will depend on when during the school year you plan to develop it (e.g., a fall newsletter should contain different information than a winter newsletter).
> *The newsletter must include headings and columns that provide an attractive format for readers.
> *The content of the newsletter should be original (not copied from a preexisting document), and it should inform readers about the various components of the program.
> *The newsletter must include at least two inserted images that are attractive and appropriate for the content.
> *A printed copy of the newsletter should be submitted to the school administrator before distribution.
> *At no time is it acceptable to copy and paste information (text, images, graphics, artwork, or sound or video files) from an Internet site into your work. This is considered plagiarism and could result in legal actions.
>
> Teacher Module 09.1 Program Newsletter
> From *Physical Education Technology Playbook* by Darla Castelli and Leah Holland Fiorentino, 2008, Champaign, IL: Human Kinetics.

Teacher Module 9.1   Program Newsletter is available to download from the companion Web site.

Teacher Module 9.2   Letter to Local Businesses

Microsoft Word templates are used in a slightly different manner in the second teacher module. Teachers write letters to local businesses promoting a new program at the school site and requesting funding for the program. The letters should express the importance of physical education and physical activity among children and adolescents and contain specific information about how the funding would facilitate the implementation of the program. Preservice teachers can place their letters in their preservice teacher portfolios to use later as professionals.

> **Teacher Module 09.2**
> **Letter to Local Businesses**
>
> **Objective**
> To write a letter to one of the local businesses to request funding to support a new physical education program you plan to start at the school.
>
> **National Standards for Beginning Physical Education Teachers**
> Standard 10 Collaboration. Understand the necessity of fostering collaborative relationships with colleagues, parents/guardians, and community agencies to support the development of a physically educated person.
>
> **Materials**
> *Computer workstations
> *Printer
> *Stamps
> *Envelopes
> *Internet connectivity
>
> **Discussion Questions**
> We know that funding from state and federal agencies is limited and that external funding is often required to start new school programs. Local businesses often support the seminal efforts to implement new programs. To convince a local business owner that there is a need for your new project, you will need to write a persuasive letter.
> *What should be included in such a letter?
> *How can you identify the local business owners that are part of the local school district area?
>
> **Tips**
> 1. Identify the positive impact the new physical education program can have on your students.
> 2. Organize your ideas into a clear, focused message that is limited to a one-page format.
> 3. Use personal experiences to support your request for funding from the business owner.
> 4. Remind the business owner about the importance of physical activity for adolescents and the impact healthy citizens can have on local businesses.
> 5. In your conclusion, restate your request for funding and invite the business owner to visit your school to see the students and speak with you directly.
> 6. The letter should include the following:
>   *Heading
>   *Dateline
>   *Inside address
>   *Salutation
>   *Body of letter
>   *Complimentary closing
>   *Your name and title
>
> Teacher Module 09.2 Letter to Local Businesses
> From *Physical Education Technology Playbook* by Darla Castelli and Leah Holland Fiorentino, 2008, Champaign, IL: Human Kinetics.

Teacher Module 9.2   Letter to Local Businesses is available to download from the companion Web site.

Lesson Plan 09.1
Sports Reporting for Newsletter
Grades 9-12

Objective
To create a newsletter that will inform others in your class and school about the success of your sport education team and share highlights from the past season.

National Standards for Physical Education
Standard 2: Demonstrates understanding of movement concepts, principles, strategies, and tactics as they apply to the learning and performance of physical activities.

Materials
*Computer workstations
*Printer
*Microsoft Publisher or Word

Accompanying File
LP09.1Student_Instructions

Set Induction
Think of your favorite sport team. Why did you start liking it? How did you find out about it? You probably learned about it through a media source such as the Internet, a newspaper, or a magazine article.

Activity
1. Place students in small groups to create a newsletter that will inform others in your class and school about the success of your sport education team and share highlights from the past season or communicate the results of a recent physically active school event (e.g., dance-a-thon, results of a tennis match, and so on).
2. Each small group will discuss the content that will be included in the newsletter. Suggest that they assign a responsibility to each person in the group, or you may decide it is better for you to assign the roles and responsibilities. For example, you might want to have a student act as a reporter and write his or her own column, such as "Brian's Blog."
3. Much of the preparatory work can be completed without a computer. Students can complete their tasks independently of the group and then bring their part to class on the day that they have access to a computer.
4. When the students are ready to put their stories, blogs, and pictures into the newsletter template, have no more than one or two students working at the computer stations at a time. The rest of the group can be doing another physical activity to avoid a lot of standing around with little to do. This step would be ideal on a laptop in the gym, but it can also be done during student free time or in a computer lab setting.
5. Remind the students to conduct a spell check and grammar check.

Lesson Plan 09.1 Sports Reporting for Newsletter   1
From *Physical Education Technology Playbook* by Darla Castelli and Leah Holland Fiorentino, 2008, Champaign, IL: Human Kinetics.

Lesson Plan 9.1 Sports Reporting for Newsletter is available to download from the companion Web site.

Lesson Plan 9.1 Sports Reporting for Newsletter

In this lesson plan, students create printed public relations materials for distribution in school settings, coaching settings, sport industry environments, or fitness sites. Specifically, they create their own physical education newsletters. Using either Microsoft Word or Microsoft Publisher, students work in small groups to create materials celebrating key events in physical education.

Lesson Plan 09.2
Letter to School Administrator
Grades 6-12

Objectives
To write a persuasive letter to your school administration or school board to convince them that the change to an optional or elective physical education program will have long-range effects that they may not have considered.

National Standards for Physical Education
Standard 5: Exhibits responsible personal and social behavior that respects self and others in physical activity settings.

Equipment
*Computer workstations
*Printer

Accompanying File
LP09.2Student_Instructions

Set Induction
Your principal and the school board have decided to change the required physical education program at your school to an optional or elective program. Because of the current obesity crisis, you are concerned about how this might limit the amount of activity that children and adolescents get each day. If physical education is eliminated, you and your friends will be able to use the normal physical education time slot for additional academic classes or for a free period. Yet, you realize that some of your friends really need to be enrolled in physical education classes because it is the only activity they get each week. You are worried about their overall health and potential future health concerns. How can you convince your principal and the school board that this is not a good idea and that students in your school need to have instructional physical activity on a regular basis to promote a physically active lifestyle in their adult lives? Principals and school board members often respond to persuasive letters written by concerned citizens of the school community.

Activity
1. Identify a school administrator and ask his or her permission to have the students complete a letter-writing assignment.
2. Obtain the mailing address of the administrator.
3. Explain to the students that a persuasive letter should contain at least a goal, reasons, and a conclusion.

Lesson Plan 09.2 Letter to School Administrator   1
From *Physical Education Technology Playbook* by Darla Castelli and Leah Holland Fiorentino, 2008, Champaign, IL: Human Kinetics.

Lesson Plans 9.2 Letter to School Administrator is available to download from the companion Web site.

Lesson Plan 9.2 Letter to School Administrator

The second lesson plan encourages students to become advocates for their own learning and to express their support for health and physical education in a letter to a school district administrator or a school board member. Combining language arts skills with technology skills and physical education subject matter, students attempt to persuade administrators to understand their point of view.

Capturing and Editing Digital Images

During computer instruction, students use the network to access a folder for their physical education class. They choose from dozens of still and video images to conduct self- and peer assessments of motor performance. Once a week you upload short video clips and several still images of game play that were recorded during class. The instructional units of team building, flag football, and tennis are saved in the physical education folder from the fall. However, for this particular assignment you have asked the students to focus on the current unit of weight training. Each student had been videotaped performing the bench press. There are also still images of other critical elements of the lifting technique (e.g., grip, distance of the bar from the chest). Students are required to view their performance and use a scoring rubric to evaluate their lifting and spotting techniques. Each student also has to evaluate the technique of his or her partner. Students typed their evaluations in a Microsoft Word template that you created and stored in the class folder. Accessing the assignment via the network, you grade and print the student work. You have used these skill analysis assignments as a quarterly project for two years now. You believe that this assignment has effectively increased student learning as well as assisted in the justification of assigning grades in physical education.

A picture is worth a thousand words. Images tell stories by capturing a period of time. They can celebrate, inspire, and generate new knowledge by providing a unique perspective on a given situation. The simple "point and shoot" nature of digital cameras has enhanced their potential for use in educational settings. This chapter focuses on capturing and editing both still and video digital images as a means of documenting student growth over time, specifically addressing NASPE teaching standards 2 (growth and development) and 8 (reflection). Capture of a single moment in time allows the teacher as well as the student to reflect on the student's performance.

Digital cameras, as opposed to those that use film, capture images in binary code, thus allowing for easy storage, deletion, and editing. They are available as stand-alone items or as accessories on cell phones or personal digital assistants (see chapter 14). The binary format allows users to preselect the quality of the image. Digital photography also permits users to rapidly send pictures via e-mail, place them on the World Wide Web (WWW), display them in a digital picture frame (a frame that reads memory cards and displays the pictures digitally), or print them, like traditional photographs. These options make it simple enough for almost everyone to assume the role of amateur photographer, sometimes without even reading the user manual that comes with the camera.

Digital video (DV) uses the binary coding system to create a higher quality of picture at more frames per second than analog video. The use of video has long been associated with the analysis of sport skills, yet some physical education teachers have been hesitant to use this technology because of a lack of time, fear of breaking the equipment, or lack of knowledge. DV allows for the repeated review of performance in slow or real time. Unlike digital still cameras, which capture single moments in time, DV captures entire events or specific segments of events. Despite requiring large amounts of storage space in a raw format, DV can easily be compressed, saved, and edited for repeated review. Whether using still or moving digital images, there has never been a better time to include multimedia to advance student learning, because images provide a perspective of one moment in time that cannot be reproduced.

DIGITAL STILL IMAGES

Digital still images are captured in pixels. The number of pixels, among other things, helps to define the picture resolution, or dpi (dots per inch). The larger the image and the greater the resolution, the greater the size of the file (output size multiplied by the resolution equals the numbers of pixels; Mohnsen, 2008). For example, a picture that is 2 inches wide and 2 inches long with 200 dpi contains 400 pixels. Before making a purchase, you will need to do your homework as some images generated from cameras housed in cell phones or personal digital assistants are hampered by small lens size, low resolution, and reduced storage space, while others are not. The safest bet is to therefore purchase stand-alone cameras separate from other handheld devices.

Physical education teachers' camera needs are different from those of other teachers. Physical educators must consider capturing moving subjects as well as having a camera that is both mobile and durable. Yet they can purchase only a digital camera that their program or school can afford. Within budget constraints, teachers should purchase cameras with the highest number of megapixels possible. Cameras with more than 5 megapixels begin to get pricey; however, by purchasing discontinued models, teachers may be able to obtain a higher quality within their price range. More megapixels do not always equal clearer photos, however; they should be considered in relation to the other features of the camera.

When purchasing a camera, teachers should also consider the type of media (memory stick) required. Cameras must be compatible with items such as printers and memory stick readers already available in the school. Teachers should purchase an additional memory stick of at least 512 megabytes. Extra batteries and a carrying case also are valuable items to consider purchasing. All of the extras will increase the amount required at the initial purchase, yet they will save time and money in the long run. Teachers may want to compare prices on the Internet to obtain the best value for the allocated budget. Many times local camera shops will match prices found on the Internet to attract local business.

Advantages of Using Digital Images

Teachers in the market for a camera should consider the advantages and disadvantages of their options. The greatest advantage of a digital camera over a film camera is the opportunity to view and delete the images immediately. A digital camera allows the teacher to confirm that the exact movement or time sequence has been captured. The short-term costs of capturing digital images are outweighed by the long-term benefits, because unwanted pictures can be deleted and better quality images preserved. Although high-quality digital cameras may cost more than 35mm cameras, when the cost of purchasing and developing film is taken into consideration, the purchase quickly becomes cost effective.

Disadvantages of Using Digital Images

There are some disadvantages associated with digital cameras, including the need to recharge batteries frequently. Another disadvantage, particularly for use during high-speed events, is the shutter delay. There is a lapse in time from when the shutter button is depressed and the picture is actually captured, sometimes resulting in missed or blurred pictures. High-speed film remains the better option for capturing high-speed images from sporting events, although professional digital cameras have minimized these concerns.

Many professional photographers argue that digital images do not have the same quality as those generated from film cameras. This is particularly evident in printed digital images that are subjected to sunlight; they fade more rapidly over time than 35 mm professional printed images do. Some counter this argument by saying that digital images are reproduced more easily than film images because film negatives react poorly to sunlight and humidity and may become brittle over time.

Critics of digital cameras also note that digital cameras may not be as durable and dependable when subjected to the elements, because they seem to react more to heat, humidity, and wet conditions. Memory sticks can also be a disadvantage, because the higher-quality and larger images require additional storage space. For most consumers, however, the advantages of digital cameras outweigh the disadvantages, because convenience and immediate access take precedence over extreme quality.

HOW TO TAKE QUALITY STILL IMAGES

As with any technology, shortcuts and techniques can enhance the quality of digital images. The quality of any photograph is determined by the surroundings. Teachers should be aware of the background of their photos, particularly when out-of-doors, being careful to avoid distractions such as parked cars and other students. A plain and simple background, such as a brick wall or a tree line, is best for capturing moving images. Teachers should experiment with backgrounds before recording student performances.

Many people are fascinated with the zoom features on cameras. They set the camera in the corner of the gymnasium, on a balcony, or in the end zone area of the playing field, then use the zoom feature to focus in on a partial aspect of play. When capturing images you want to get as close as possible to the image. Overzooming can cause blurring of the picture, as the camera becomes oversensitive to any movement, even a slight sway.

Teachers also need to be aware of lighting. Reduced light or the presence of shadows may require the use of a flash. They should also consider distance between the camera and the student because it will affect the quality of the image; if the camera is too far from the student for the flash to adequately reach, the images might be dark, blurry, or both. When outside, teachers should stand with the sun at their backs before taking pictures.

Today, digital cameras and computers often come with digital still image editing software. This software allows the editor to remove red eyes and resize, blur, crop, and layer the image. The selection of the software depends on the needs of the user. Teachers who simply want to take pictures and view the images "as is" will be happy with the software that comes with the camera. Those who want to manipulate the images extensively may choose to use more sophisticated software, such as Adobe Photoshop. Despite the availability of editing software, however, the quality of the image is determined during the capture process. If a captured image is poor, no editing software can substantially increase the quality.

DIGITAL VIDEO IMAGES

The recommendations for capturing quality DV images are similar to those for still images, yet some are worth reiterating. Deciding on the right digital video camera can be difficult because so many choices are available. The price the teacher can afford to pay, the type of media, and the quality of the image all should be considered before purchasing a camcorder. Because many video cameras come with unnecessary features, teachers should create a list of necessary features prior to shopping. A carrying case, batteries, and an extra memory stick (because digital video cameras can also capture still images) should be included in the initial purchase. To capture quality images, the camcorder should be placed in a stable position. With DV this is even more important than with still images. We recommend using a tripod whenever possible. This should also be part of the initial purchase, which will affect the cost.

Teachers must choose which form of media will be best for their needs. The mini DV tape format is presently the most popular, but physical education teachers have other choices now as well. Teachers should first consider the purpose of capturing the video (e.g., preparing video for the WWW without editing or editing the video in segments). For teachers who do not want to do much editing, we recommend a disk-based camera that stores the video immediately to a DVD or video CD. Disk-based camcorders can record between 20 minutes and 1 hour of **MPEG** video (depending on the quality selection) directly to small DVDs that can then be played in standard DVD players. Teachers interested in editing or transferring the video to a PC for storage may prefer a tape-based camcorder. MPEG in all its forms is first and foremost a delivery format, which makes it less than ideal for editing on a PC.

Whether the digital video camera is disk based or tape based, the DV should be captured at a rate of 30 frames per second, with proper lighting, and as close to the subject as possible. Video recorded at 30 frames per second retains its quality during playback in slow motion with little dropping of frames (which looks like a glitch). The quality of DV is affected by how the light shines on the lens of the camera as well as how much light is present. Unlike digital still cameras, users cannot just simply turn on the flash and increase the amount of light. Teachers will need to experiment to find the area of the gymnasium that allows them to capture the highest-quality DV.

Because DV cannot be rotated in the editing process the way still images can, the camera should always remain upright, not on its side, during the capture phase. Teachers should minimize the use of the zoom feature on the camera, taking advantage of this feature only when necessary (e.g., when attempting to focus on the hands or feet of the subject). The bottom line is that teachers need to capture the highest-quality DV possible, because editing software will not be able to increase its quality. Specifics on the editing of DV are discussed in chapter 12.

WHY USE DIGITAL IMAGING IN PHYSICAL EDUCATION?

Digital images can enhance instruction, help students understand tactics and strategies, motivate students to excel, provide new information, and expand students' perspectives. Digital images can be placed in PowerPoint presentations to increase the impact on the audience. Displaying an image of a cancerous lung, for example, is far more provocative than simply talking to students about the dangers of smoking.

Students have reported that they are more motivated when task explanations include images. Visual learners especially profit from the presence of images on task cards, worksheets, examinations, directions, and bulletin boards. In addition, images of peers can have a greater impact on student learning than images of professional athletes. The presence of images, particularly of their peers, makes the task seem doable.

As an example, the concept of open space is difficult to teach students, because they are often unaware of its existence. The use of images can help students identify open space by identifying where the opponents and teammates are located. In the vignette at the beginning of this chapter, students viewed both still and video images to assess their own performance and that of their peers. If one of the scoring criteria were to be moving into open space or creating open space, the students could use the images to identify whether this indeed occurred.

Images also facilitate learning when a teacher is unable to present an ideal demonstration of a performance. They also enable teachers to provide alternative viewing angles. The camera can capture images from multiple angles, providing information that could not be generated any other way. When this information is presented as feedback immediately following a performance, it can help to augment the quality of movement (Rink, 2005). Images alone, void of verbal feedback from the teacher, are usually not enough to change movement patterns; yet when presented in concert, they can be very effective. This idea also holds true for teachers who use digital images to evaluate their own teaching, and when combined with a critical eye, these images can increase the likelihood of effective teaching.

SUMMARY

Digital still and video images can enhance student learning and teacher effectiveness in physical education because images inspire action. Whether capturing a single point or multiple points in time, images can help both teachers and students review and analyze performances. Digital images can help teachers who have not developed an expertise in movement analysis become adequate evaluators, particularly when they are given scoring criteria and minimal training. Teachers purchasing digital image equipment should be sure to stay within the school budget and purchase only after conducting a needs assessment.

LEARNING MODULES

The learning modules are available to download from the companion Web site at www.HumanKinetics.com/PhysicalEducationTechnologyPlaybook.

Teacher Module 10.1
Reciprocal Teaching Assessment

Objective
To capture quality digital video (DV) of a teaching episode and conduct a systematic observation analysis to evaluate the teaching performance.

National Standards for Beginning Physical Education Teachers
Standard 8 Reflection. Understand the importance of being a reflective practitioner and its contribution to overall professional development and actively seek opportunities to sustain professional growth.

Materials
*Digital video cameras
*Batteries
*CDs or tapes
*Tripods
*Extension cords
*Microphone (optional)

Discussion Question
What is systematic observation, and how it can be used to improve teaching effectiveness?

Directions
1. Plan a lesson for K-12 students. Organize the learning environment to accommodate a videotaping session; make sure you have cameras, batteries, tapes or CDs, tripods, and extension cords. Secure parental permission prior to videotaping the lesson (see chapter 2).
2. Capture your entire teaching session on videotape from multiple angles and as close to the students as possible (to allow for quality footage and acceptable audio levels), but do not interfere with the lesson itself. Remember to confirm that the camera is actually recording the event. This can usually be done by observing a red light on the camera or by replaying a brief initial practice video clip. (Hint: For this evaluation, it may be best to wear a microphone during the videotaping.)
3. Store the video in a safe place until it can be replayed.
4. Choose one of the systematic observation criteria methods and use it to evaluate the teaching episode.
5. Write a self-evaluation of your teaching performance during lesson instruction.

Systematic Observation 1
Watch the videotape to evaluate your ability to monitor your students during the entire lesson. Choose three 5-minute time periods. During each time period, you will mark each 15-second duration in which you may have turned your back to one or more students.

Teacher Module 10.1 Reciprocal Teaching Assessment   1
From *Physical Education Technology Playbook* by Darla Castelli and Leah Holland Fiorentino, 2008, Champaign, IL: Human Kinetics.

Teacher Module 10.1 Reciprocal Teaching Assessment is available to download from the companion Web site.

Teacher Module 10.1   Reciprocal Teaching Assessment

Teachers teaching teachers can be an effective way to improve the quality of instruction. The first teacher module requires teachers to capture and systematically code a segment of a peer's teaching. They then make recommendations for improving teaching effectiveness. DV allows for repeated viewing in real time and slow motion. During each viewing teachers can focus on different elements, such as the amount of feedback provided by the teacher, the teacher's location and proximity to the students, or the students' level of engagement during the task.

Teacher Module 10.2
Digital Assessment

Objective
To use a DVD-R recorder and video camera to provide specific, congruent feedback to students performing a motor skill.

National Standards for Beginning Physical Education Teachers
Standard 2 Growth and Development. Understand how individuals learn and develop, and provide opportunities that support physical, cognitive, social, and emotional development.

Materials
*Digital video cameras
*DVD-R recorder
*RCA or firewire cables

Discussion Questions
*How can teachers implement video technology and still respect the rights of others?
*How does immediate feedback about performance affect student achievement?

Directions
1. Choose an instructional unit that has a strong skill component (the skill will be broken down into its components and the students will need to be given ample practice time). We suggest a swimming unit, in which each person in class will learn the basic swimming stroke called freestyle.
2. By the far lane of the pool, set up a video camera near the starter's block to capture images of the students' freestyle stroke. The video camera should be on a rolling cart and plugged into a DVD-R recording device (a DVD version of a VCR). The video footage is actually being captured on the DVD-R for replay on a DVD player, not the video camera.
3. Organize the environment so that three to five students swim in this lane for two lengths of the pool while the video is being captured.
4. Move the video camera to the side of the pool to capture the swim stroke from a different angle or side view.
5. The students again swim two lengths of the pool. After two lengths, the students rotate to a different swim lane and the process begins again.
6. Explain to the students that they will be assessed on their freestyle technique and reiterate the critical element you expect to observe.
7. The DV is stored on DVD for quick review on a DVD player by the teacher or the students.
8. Create an evaluation sheet for the students' swimming technique to give to each student.

Teacher Module 10.2 Digital Assessment   1
From *Physical Education Technology Playbook* by Darla Castelli and Leah Holland Fiorentino, 2008, Champaign, IL: Human Kinetics.

Teacher Module 10.2 Digital Assessment is available to download from the companion Web site.

Teacher Module 10.2   Digital Assessment

The second teacher module requires teachers to use a video camera that records to DVD-R to capture images of a motor skill performance such as the freestyle swim stroke. By capturing the video in this format, teachers can immediately place the video into a DVD player for review. No editing is required, so teachers can quickly review students' performances. The replay and slow-motion features should help teachers in their performance assessment.

Lesson Plan 10.1 Digital Still Assessment

The first lesson plan requires students to create their own criteria sheets for specific movements or skills. They then have to capture still images of these elements to use in self-evaluations and peer evaluations.

Lesson Plan 10.1
Digital Still Assessment
Grades 9-12

Objective
To create a criteria sheet for a particular movement or skill and to assess a peer based on still images and photos that have captured the movement or skill.

National Standards for Physical Education
Standard 1: Demonstrates competency in motor skills and movement patterns needed to perform a variety of physical activities.

Materials
*Computer workstations
*Digital cameras
*Firewire cable

Accompanying File
LP10.1Student_Instructions

Set Induction
A picture is worth a thousand words! Many photographers in the past have caught some pretty unbelievable pictures with their cameras. Imagine seeing yourself on the cover of a sport magazine—you'll want to make sure you are performing the skill correctly. By using still images, you can see your motor skill technique. Can still images help you become motor competent?

Activity
1. As the teacher, you can choose a sport skill in one of the units of your curriculum (e.g., golf swing, tennis serve, swim stroke, and so on) for the students to break down using digital images, or you can have the students select one skill from the current unit that you are teaching. If this is the first time that you are using the term *critical elements of movement* with your students, choose a familiar task, such as throwing a ball.
2. The students will then create a list of the important parts of that skill such as grip, approach, and follow through. You will need to decide if you want the students to capture the digital images or if you want to use the camera and upload the images to the computer (see Teaching Tips).
3. Determine how the students will work in partners.
4. Gain access to a laptop computer or computer laboratory to allow the students to insert their images into a word processing file.
5. Be sure to keep the students focused on the accurate identification of the critical elements of the movement.

Lesson Plan 10.1 Digital Still Assessment 1
From *Physical Education Technology Playbook* by Darla Castelli and Leah Holland Fiorentino, 2008, Champaign, IL: Human Kinetics.

Lesson Plan 10.1 Digital Still Assessment is available to download from the companion Web site.

Lesson Plan 10.2 Illustrating an Understanding of Movement Concepts

The second lesson plan moves beyond identification and requires students to demonstrate an understanding of a movement pattern or principle. Using educational gymnastics and the concept of balance, students perform a variety of balance skills that are recorded by their classmates in the form of digital still images. The images are then used as samples to illustrate student understanding of key concepts related to the movement or principle.

Lesson Plan 10.2
Illustrating an Understanding of Movement Concepts
Grades 4-8

Objective
To understand the concepts of balance, unbalance, counterbalance, and countertension using still images.

National Standards for Physical Education
Standard 1: Demonstrates competency in motor skills and movement patterns needed to perform a variety of physical activities.
Standard 2: Demonstrates understanding of movement concepts, principles, strategies, and tactics as they apply to the learning and performance of physical activities.

Materials
*Computer workstations
*Firewire cable
*Digital still cameras

Accompanying File
LP10.2Student_Instructions

Set Induction
What does it look like when one person is balancing? What are the characteristics of balance? Is the person still or moving? Is the body tight or loose? Are parts of the body straight? If two people are touching each other, what would it look like if they were balanced? What would it look like if they were unbalanced? What is counterbalance? What is countertension?

Activity
1. This lesson provides an opportunity to integrate technology into your educational gymnastics unit. Specifically, you will need to help the students understand and practice the concepts of counterbalance and countertension. "In a counter-balance position the gymnast's center of gravity is outside the base of support, but by pushing against another gymnast or supporting one's weight with or against a piece of equipment, a stable balance position is achieved" (Werner, 1994, p. 24). A countertension balance focuses on the pulling away as "two or more gymnasts are pulling away from each other with their center of gravity outside of their base" to achieve a balance (Werner, 1994, p. 24).
2. Once these concepts have been introduced, assign the students the task of practicing them in small groups chosen either by yourself or by the students. The students should be able to come up with at least one balance reflecting counterbalance and one demonstrating countertension.

Lesson Plan 10.2 Illustrating an Understanding of Movement Concepts 1
From *Physical Education Technology Playbook* by Darla Castelli and Leah Holland Fiorentino, 2008, Champaign, IL: Human Kinetics.

Lesson Plan 10.2 Illustrating an Understanding of Movement Concepts is available to download from the companion Web site.

Advanced Microsoft PowerPoint

Before class begins, you carefully affix 10 basketball performance criteria sheets to the walls of the gymnasium. You have planned a lesson in which the students will use a self-check style to practice several ball-handling tasks. They will practice the tasks at learning stations, stopping frequently to correct or reinforce their performances. Because you premade the criteria sheets using presentation software, you are now free to monitor the students and ensure that they refine their skill by pausing to reflect about their own performances in relation to the criteria sheets. This style of teaching in combination with the use of technology has both increased teacher efficiency and improved student performance.

Preservice teachers have identified Microsoft PowerPoint as the software application that has the greatest potential for integration into physical education curricula because of its versatility. Microsoft PowerPoint aids teachers in the creation of presentations, handouts, interactive animation, stand-alone kiosks, task cards, and Web pages to deliver information to students in a visually effective and high-speed fashion. According to Hancock, Bray, and Nason (2002), enhanced, authentic multimedia can motivate students, accommodate large groups, and deliver information dynamically to visual learners. This chapter helps teachers refine their skills related to NASPE teaching standards 1 (content knowledge), 6 (planning and instruction), and 7 (student assessment) through the use of advanced Microsoft PowerPoint techniques. Although the chapter begins with some basic functions of the software, the focal point is the advanced features that are specific to the needs of physical education teachers. Despite the chapter's focus on a specific software, many of these features are similar in other presentation software (i.e., Macintosh KeyNote).

The unique characteristic of this software is that it is user-friendly for people of all ages, thus permitting both teachers and students to create Microsoft PowerPoint products such as presentations. Students can prepare presentations for their peers, make interactive storybooks, or create posters displaying their knowledge. Microsoft PowerPoint, a high-impact teaching tool for the start of the 21st century, is noted for its potential to increase social learning, enhance content, and facilitate student learning.

HOW TO USE MICROSOFT POWERPOINT

Microsoft PowerPoint is as simple as click and type. The best way for a novice user to learn how to use Microsoft PowerPoint is to try all of the features located on the top toolbar. To get started, the teacher should open the software and select *File,* then *New.* The teacher must then decide what product to create. If she wants to create a presentation, she can choose a blank presentation template or a design template (see figure 11.1). Hundreds of design templates are available from within the software itself and through online resources. Many have educational or sport-related themes. Ambitious teachers may choose to design their own templates.

Inserting text is simple; the teacher only has to select the text box that appears on the screen and begin to type. Because the software is part of the Microsoft Office suite, it has many of the tools of a word processor, such as spelling and grammar checks. As with all Microsoft products, these tools are included on the top toolbar. By changing the slide layout, a teacher can reformat the appearance of the text on the document. Several slide layouts can be found under *Format* (on the top toolbar). Once the text appears on the screen, the teacher

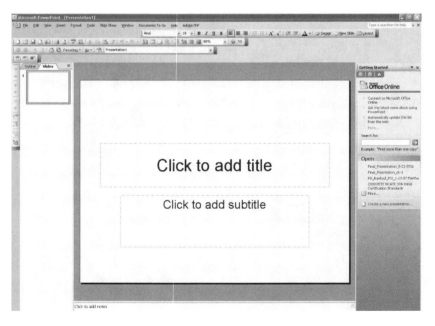

Figure 11.1 Image of new Microsoft PowerPoint file.

Microsoft Office PowerPoint screenshot reprinted with permission from Microsoft Corporation.

will need to save the file as a presentation, thus allowing her to modify the presentation as needed. As the teacher further develops the presentation, she must continually save the updated materials.

The text embedded in the presentation is ready to be displayed on the gymnasium wall by using a computer and LCD projector. It can also be printed as a handout for students. It is important to limit the number of words linked together to avoid information overload. The text on a presentation slide is not meant to require extensive reading; because it should be more of an outline or overview, it should be brief. A bulleted point should contain approximately seven words and should not be written as a complete sentence. To print the information on the slides, the teacher selects *File,* then *Print* (on the top toolbar). Within the print menu she will need to select what to print (she can choose from slides, handouts, note pages, or an outline). By selecting *Print Preview,* the teacher can decide which display would best meet students' needs.

Adding Graphics

Graphics and images can enhance presentations. To add clipart to the presentation, the teacher selects *Insert,* then *Pictures* (on the top toolbar). The teacher can choose clipart from Microsoft PowerPoint or from another media file on the computer. Microsoft also offers clipart online. Tables, graphics, and Microsoft Excel spreadsheets can also be integrated into the presentation if needed. (These features are located on the toolbar under *Insert,* the same location for picture insertion.)

Having located an image, graphic, or table to include in the presentation, the teacher then selects *Insert.* The object can then be relocated by clicking and dragging it or resized by pulling on the corners. The picture will default to an open space in the presentation, but its position can easily be modified.

Duplicate or new slides are added to the presentation by selecting *Insert* (on the top toolbar). Slides can be managed from a slide icon in the left-hand column, from the outline, or by actually viewing the slide show. The *Slide Sorter* view option allows users to manage large presentations containing many slides. From this view, the slide order can be adjusted by clicking and dragging.

Advanced Elements

Microsoft PowerPoint presentations can also contain video and sound or be saved in a variety of formats. A Microsoft PowerPoint slide that includes a video can be modified for use with a number of classes. A text-only presentation is small and can usually be saved on a USB flash drive or network. The size of the file increases as images (especially video) and interactive elements (such as buttons) are added to the presentation. Issues related to storing large files are minor compared to the benefits associated with the inclusion of multimedia.

Adding Multimedia to the Presentation

The term *multimedia* refers to the collective use of text, graphics, animation, and video in a single forum to deliver information to a specific audience. It also refers to the use of computers to create or generate these materials. Multimedia, when not overdone, can enhance student learning by increasing self-efficacy (Bandura, 1997). Hyperlinks embedded in the text of the presentation can link to URLs or video files such as MPEG, AVI, or MOV. Similar to the hyperlinks on a Web page, they create a connection to information beyond the presentation, thus embellishing the content for the learner.

To create a hyperlink, the teacher first selects a text box on the presentation slide. Next, the teacher selects *Insert,* then *Hyperlink* (top toolbar), opening the hyperlink menu. From the menu, the teacher enters the text to view on the screen, as well as locates the file or URL to be connected. The teacher should realize that the hyperlink will not work immediately because it is functional only when the slide show is in the viewing function.

Teachers have the option of embedding a video into the presentation slide or leaving the presentation to show a video. Only MPEG and AVI (analog video) files can be embedded into Microsoft PowerPoint slides. This is done using the *Insert* function. The teacher should note that the image size can be increased, but doing so will likely distort it.

Once the teacher has all of the content, text, graphics, and images on the slides, it is time to consider how the slide show will be managed by the presenter. To view the slide show, the teacher can use the F5 key. This causes the software application to close, filling the monitor screen with the slide. At this point each slide is advanced by clicking the mouse or pressing the space bar on the keyboard. The letter *p* on the keyboard is used to return to the previous slide.

To set up transitions between slides or embed animation into the presentation, the teacher selects *Slide Show* and then *Slide Show Transitions* or *Custom Animations.* The custom animation feature allows selected parts of slides to have staggered entrances.

For example, the first line of the text may appear and then change color on a mouse click as the next line of text appears. The preview window allows the teacher to see how the transition or animation looks. Teachers should remember that with these features, less is more. Transitions and animation can be distracting to viewers and should be used only to increase comprehension.

Interactive and Stand-Alone Presentations

Like Web pages, Microsoft PowerPoint presentations can be designed in a linear (step-by-step) format or a nonlinear format, in which the user determines the order of navigation. Interactive and stand-alone presentations are designed to be used when the teacher cannot be present (e.g., when the presentation is online or used at a learning station in the gym or at a kiosk). Using the action buttons *(Slide Show)*, a teacher can create a quiz game to help students review for a cognitive test.

Stand-alone presentations are those that transition to the next slide without a mouse click. On the slide transition menu, the teacher can elect to have the presentation advance to the next slide after a specified period of time or automatically after five seconds (see figure 11.2). When this feature is used in conjunction with music or sound, the slides automatically advance throughout the song.

Figure 11.2 Types of slide transitions.

The teacher can project a presentation on the wall of the gymnasium to increase motivation or run a presentation from a laptop on a rolling cart in the corner or from a handheld device (see chapter 14) as an interactive learning station.

USING POWERPOINT TO ENHANCE LEARNING

Teachers can use Microsoft PowerPoint to foster learning in K-12 students by creating presentations, pictures, task cards, posters, and Web pages. Teachers should employ a variety of teaching styles to facilitate student learning. Those styles range from direct to indirect teaching, with some presentations resulting in more physical activity than others. A formal classroom presentation may be in order to set the stage for student activity. Microsoft PowerPoint presentations are ideal for presenting safety issues or new information. They can also be used by the classroom teacher to have physical activity breaks (www.take10.net).

Once the teacher has identified the key content for a Microsoft PowerPoint presentation, she should create a title slide, a slide providing an overview of the presentation, and several logically sequenced slides containing the essential information. The presentation should conclude with a slide that summarizes all of the materials covered. Using the print feature, the teacher could provide handouts for students to take home. It is extremely important that the teacher not read the slides during the presentation. Rather, she should emphasize each point on the slides or highlight only a few pieces of information and then expand the content. Poor communication skills can adversely affect well-planned and well-prepared PowerPoint presentations.

Task Cards, Pictures, and Posters

Microsoft PowerPoint can be used to create slides to serve as task cards, pictures, or posters. Task cards are created by simply following the previously outlined directions for the inclusion of text and images on a slide. Each slide can be printed on an 8.5 × 11 inch or larger piece of paper. There are several advantages to using this software to create task cards rather than paper and pencil: *(1)* professional appearance, *(2)* preservation for future use or modification, *(3)* print options (can be printed with a color printer or on color paper with black ink), and *(4)* reduced preparation time.

Any slide can be printed and saved as a JPEG file (see chapter 6). To save a presentation, the teacher selects *Save As* and then the type of format. If JPEG is selected as the file type, it will be stored as a picture. Once saved as a JPEG, this image can be altered only through the use of photo editing software. This feature is important when developing advanced multimedia editing (described in chapter 12). This format is of particular value for the creation of Web pages or other media for teaching.

The printing of posters or banners requires an oversized printer, which the school district may or may not own. To turn a presentation slide into a poster, the teacher must customize the size of the page. In the *Print* menu, the teacher can increase the size of the slide to the limit of the paper size in the printer. Banners and posters can contribute to the creation of a positive learning environment in the gymnasium as well as throughout the school.

Presentations as Web Pages

As described in chapter 6, Web pages can play an important role in physical education programs. Although Web development is not a primary function of Microsoft PowerPoint, it can serve as a functional way to get information to the Web quickly and easily. The user simply creates the presentation using a template and then saves the template as a Web page. The conversion to HTML is done by the software. All of the presentation's slides and links are stored in a Web folder on the hard drive. Once the Web page is created, it is best to use HTML editing software to edit the content. The final product is interactive and allows the viewer to navigate the content in a nonlinear fashion.

SUMMARY

Microsoft PowerPoint is a versatile program that can be integrated easily into physical education classes and programs. It can be used to create banners, posters, Web pages, presentations, pictures, task cards, and displays for freestanding kiosks to improve teacher efficiency and enhance learning. This software has something of value for both teachers and students, whether they are accessing a design template or creating a template through the use of advanced functions. Presentations can be compelling and persuasive, but more important is the intent to communicate a deeper understanding of a body of knowledge, not simply to entertain an audience.

LEARNING MODULES

The learning modules are available to download from the companion Web site at www.HumanKinetics.com/PhysicalEducationTechnologyPlaybook.

Teacher Module 11.1
Content Knowledge

Objective
To create a PowerPoint presentation that demonstrates mastery of basic features of the software, such as inserting graphics and animation.

National Standards for Beginning Physical Education Teachers
*Standard 1 Content Knowledge. Understand physical education content and disciplinary concepts related to the development of a physically educated person.
*Standard 6 Planning and Instruction. Understand the importance of planning developmentally appropriate instructional units to foster the development of a physically educated person.

Materials
*Computer workstations
*Microsoft PowerPoint

Discussion Questions
*What is knowledge?
*How can we share knowledge?
*With whom should we share knowledge?

Directions

Note: All of the figures were taken from PowerPoint XP. PowerPoint 95, 98, and 2000 each look a little different, but the functions and language has remained the same.

1. Open PowerPoint and select *Blank Presentation* (see figure 11.1).
2. Select *Design*.
3. Select *New Slide*.
4. Create at least eight slides with content related to the specific topic by selecting *Insert*, then *New or Duplicate Slides*. Remember that these slides should reflect your knowledge of content.
5. The first slide is a title slide. The last slide is your conclusion slide. Create six slides between your title slide and conclusion slide.
6. Save the file with an appropriate name in an appropriate drive.

Applying a Design Template
1. Select *Format*.
2. Select *Slide Design*.
3. From the toolbar in the right column, select a color scheme or a design template.

Teacher Module 11.1 Content Knowledge   1
From *Physical Education Technology Playbook* by Darla Castelli and Leah Holland Fiorentino, 2008, Champaign, IL: Human Kinetics.

Teacher Module 11.1 Content Knowledge is available to download from the companion Web site.

Teacher Module 11.1   Content Knowledge

The first teacher module requires the creation of a Microsoft PowerPoint presentation that focuses on the mastery of basic features of the software, such as inserting graphics and animation. At the completion of this module, teachers will be able to create a presentation using visual media, reflecting knowledge of specific content, for a variety of audiences and purposes.

Teacher Module 11.2
Motor Skill Instruction Project

Objective
To create a presentation that will introduce students to the critical elements of a specific motor skill. For successful completion of this module, prerequisite skills are contained in chapter 10. More specifically, teachers should be able to capture a video clip and save it in an MPEG format.

National Standards for Beginning Physical Education Teachers
*Standard 5 Communication. Use knowledge of effective verbal, nonverbal, and media communication techniques to enhance learning and engagement in physical activity settings.
*Standard 7 Student Assessment. Understand and use the varied types of assessment and their contribution to the overall program and the development of the physical, cognitive, social, and emotional domains.

Materials
*Computer workstations
*Digital still cameras
*Digital video cameras
*Microsoft PowerPoint
*CD-R or CD-R/W

Discussion Questions
*Orally list the progression of tasks in a lesson plan for a specific motor skill for eighth-grade students.
*What new skills or attitudes will the students acquire from the tasks?
*Why did you choose to include these tasks in the lesson?

Directions
1. Obtain permission from parents to photograph students completing a specific motor task (e.g., volleyball set or tennis serve). Capture several digital images of a specific motor skill (e.g., a tennis serve). Save these images in a folder on the desktop of the computer.
2. Add photos to the Microsoft PowerPoint presentation.
   a. Open Microsoft PowerPoint.
   b. Select *Insert*, and click *Pictures* from the top toolbar.
   c. Select *From File*.
   d. Select *View*, point to *Master*, and then click *Slide Master* from the top toolbar.
   e. Insert the graphic (a photo, drawing, auto shape, WordArt, clipart, or another type of picture) you want to use for your watermark.
   f. Size and edit the graphic to suit your needs.
   g. If you inserted a WordArt or auto shape object, use a solid light color for the fill and do not use any fill effects (such as gradient or textured).
3. Add WordArt to the PowerPoint presentation.

Teacher Module 11.2 Motor Skill Instruction Project
From *Physical Education Technology Playbook* by Darla Castelli and Leah Holland Fiorentino, 2008, Champaign, IL: Human Kinetics.   1

Teacher Module 11.2 Motor Skill Instruction Project is available to download from the companion Web site.

Teacher Module 11.2   Motor Skill Instruction Project

The second teacher module requires the teacher to use advanced features of Microsoft PowerPoint to link to video. This module also encourages teachers to add graphics, leading to developing skills necessary for template design or the creation of an original template. This module also advances teachers' video capture and editing skills as they are introduced to the necessary skills to place the media into a user-friendly presentation format.

Lesson Plan 11.1 Inspector Graphic

The first lesson plan in this chapter requires the students to use Microsoft PowerPoint to design a physical activity program for someone their age. Students will review a Fitnessgram/Activitygram report and create a program based on the strengths and weaknesses described in the report. The slides should include the type, frequency, duration, and intensity of the physical activities, along with weekly recommendations and fitness goals.

Lesson Plan 11.1
Inspector Graphic
Grades 9-10

Objective
To create a Microsoft PowerPoint presentation containing a six-week physical activity program that is based on a Fitnessgram/Activitygram report.

National Standards for Physical Education
*Standard 2: Demonstrates understanding of movement concepts, principles, strategies, and tactics as they apply to the learning and performance of physical activities.
*Standard 4: Achieves and maintains a health-enhancing level of physical fitness.

Materials
*Computer workstations
*Digital still cameras
*Microsoft PowerPoint
*Results from a fitness test such as Fitnessgram/Activitygram

Accompanying File
LP11.1Student_Instructions

Set Induction
What is problem-based learning? How can you help others solve problems related to physical activity or fitness?

Activity
1. Provide the students with a copy of a Fitnessgram/Activitygram report of a student of similar age. Make sure the report reflects clear health-related fitness strengths and weaknesses. For example, Jolanda completed only 10 laps on the PACER test when in fact she should have completed 23 to be in the Healthy Fitness Zone, thus suggesting that she needs to address her cardiorespiratory fitness.
2. Be sure the students have an understanding of each health-related fitness component (cardiorespiratory endurance, muscular endurance, body composition, strength, and flexibility) before distributing the student instructions. The students should also understand which Fitnessgram test measures each health-related fitness component.
3. Students should also be familiar with the FITT principle (frequency, intensity, time, and type of activities) in relation to their age group.
4. After you give out the instructions, have the students work in pairs to identify the strengths and weaknesses of the report and to identify how active someone in their age group should be.
5. The students should then determine which activities would likely be most beneficial for the individual identified in the report.

Lesson Plan 11.1 Inspector Graphic   1
From *Physical Education Technology Playbook* by Darla Castelli and Leah Holland Fiorentino, 2008, Champaign, IL: Human Kinetics.

Lesson Plan 11.1 Inspector Graphic is available to download from the companion Web site.

Lesson Plan 11.2 There Is No "I" in TEAM

The second lesson plan in this chapter requires students to use Microsoft PowerPoint to demonstrate their understanding of good sporting behavior. Working in groups, students in grades 3-5 identify how they should behave as members of a team or in a physical activity setting. They use Microsoft PowerPoint to create miniposters that display keywords or slogans about positive behaviors in a physical activity setting.

Lesson Plan 11.2
There Is No "I" in TEAM
Grades 3-5

Objective
To create a poster that promotes good sporting behavior.

National Standards for Physical Education
*Standard 5: Exhibits responsible personal and social behavior that respects self and others in physical activity settings.
*Standard 6: Values physical activity for health, enjoyment, challenge, self-expression, and/or social interaction.

Materials
*Computer workstations
*Microsoft PowerPoint
*Printer

Accompanying File
LP11.2Student_Instructions

Set Induction
What makes a group of people a team? How should team members behave? What is good sporting behavior? Why is it important?

Activity
1. Have the students brainstorm about fair play and good sporting behavior.
2. Generate a list of socially responsible behaviors. Display this list at the front of the computer lab.
3. Get the students into groups of three. Make sure you work out a rotation so that everyone gets a chance to use the keyboard and the mouse. This is important with this age group.
4. Have Microsoft PowerPoint open and ask the students to move their mouse so the screensaver closes and a blank page in Microsoft PowerPoint appears.
5. Allow the students to type some words and show them how to change colors and design templates.
6. Have the students save their work and then have them print their posters. Before printing, you will need to select *File* and *Page Setup* to identify how large you want to print the posters. You will be limited by the size of your printer.
7. Suggest that each student make a poster.

Lesson Plan 11.2 There Is No "I" in TEAM   1
From *Physical Education Technology Playbook* by Darla Castelli and Leah Holland Fiorentino, 2008, Champaign, IL: Human Kinetics.

Lesson Plan 11.2 There Is No "I" in TEAM is available to download from the companion Web site.

Advanced Editing and Multimedia Production

Over the summer you took a trip to Finland and had an opportunity to participate in several Finnish sport-related activities including folk dance, skittles, and Finnish baseball. You wanted to share these experiences with your students on the first of day of classes, so you took digital still and video images and created a digital story of your experiences. The video lasted only four minutes but encapsulated the history of the sports by including traditional music, text, and pictures, to mention just a few of the possible media. The video stimulated class discussion about the lives of Finnish people. One student, who noticed a McDonald's sign in the background of the video, wanted to know whether obesity is as much of an issue in Finland as it is in the United States. Although you had hoped that the discussion would focus on sport history and culture, the idea that these media inspired this depth of dialogue convinced you that this is something you need to do more often.

This chapter attempts to address NASPE teaching standards 3 (diverse learners) and 6 (planning and instruction) through the creation of multimedia projects. The term *multimedia,* as discussed in chapter 11, refers to the integration of text, graphics, animation, and video in a single forum to deliver information to a specific audience. It can also refer to the use of computers to create or generate these materials. When used in concert to elicit emotion, these media can create dramatic stories. *Digital storytelling* is a relatively new term used to describe a narrative that contains various electronic elements to enhance delivery. It is not necessary to be the star of the video; digital storytelling emphasizes that everyone matters and even the quietest member of the group can have a voice by creating a dramatic presentation that elicits emotions through the use of images and music. This student-centered approach to learning draws on personal experiences and events to connect people.

Because multimedia presentations often look and feel authentic, students respond more intensely to them than they do to traditional teaching strategies. For example, a teacher can prepare a history presentation about World War II as a multimedia production about the Holocaust containing artifacts such as a brief interview with the granddaughter of a survivor, pictures, an audio clip of a student reading from *The Diary of Anne Frank,* and black-and-white photos to make the audience feel as though they were there. Yet, to tell a story using digital media, one must possess digital video (DV) capture and editing skills. This chapter focuses on the editing of DV, building on the skills necessary for image capturing as discussed in chapter 10.

CAPTURING DIGITAL VIDEO

The companies Apple, Sony, and Microsoft progressively encouraged the use of DV editing, moving it into the mainstream by including editing software with the purchase of computers. Apple's iMovie, one of the first editing software programs to be widely available, is among the easiest to use. Its advantage is that the movie is saved in a MOV format that can be played back using QuickTime on either platform of computer (Macintosh or PC). The QuickTime player allows the user to manipulate playback by changing screen size, relocating the player on the screen, or streaming the movie on the Internet. The disadvantage is that not all teachers have access to Macintosh computers. We recommend iMovie over other DV editing software; however, many of the features that will be described in this chapter are available in all software formats.

Windows Movie Maker, which comes with all versions of Windows 2000 or later, brought DV editing to the PC. Because there are more PC users than Macintosh users, Windows Media Player and Windows Movie Maker are more in the mainstream than iMovie is. The disadvantage of Windows Movie Maker is that it has limited playback capability. For example, in general, movies created with Windows Movie Maker cannot be played back on Macintosh computers. Whether using a Macintosh or Windows-based computer, plenty of options are available to edit captured video.

When authoring multimedia productions, teachers must begin with the end in mind. By asking themselves, "Who is the target audience, and what do I want them to see, learn, and experience from the multimedia?" they can then plan backward. For physical education teachers, the target audience is clear, but age appropriateness is not. What may be effective for 9-year-olds is boring to 15-year-olds. One easy way for teachers to address age appropriateness is by including the audience's peers in the video.

By planning backward, teachers are more likely to meet the needs of their audiences if they have predetermined what to capture, collected more video than needed, and identified all potential artifacts. The author who grabs the camera without a plan and starts capturing video often has to go back and recapture more footage because what she collected was inadequate or inappropriate. The effective multimedia author plans using these steps: (1) identify the audience, (2) create the storyboard, (3) capture the video, (4) edit the video, and (5) produce and evaluate the presentation.

One way to organize a plan for a multimedia presentation is to create a storyboard. A storyboard is like a blank comic strip (see table 12.1, or figure 6.1 on page 35). The teacher begins by placing text in each cell, which represents a movie scene. Then she develops these ideas to include more detail such as images, teaching cues, text, and sound. In these initial phases, the teacher should not be concerned with transitions between

TABLE 12.1   Storyboard

Introduction to salsa dance	Demonstration of a step sequence	Breakdown of part 1 of sequence	Breakdown of part 2 of sequence	Demonstration of an authentic salsa dance

scenes, theme colors, or fonts, but rather with camera angles and shots to capture.

From the storyboard, the teacher makes a list of screen shots, which represents what to capture using the video camera. Teachers should always capture more footage than actually required to avoid the need to recreate the scene and capture additional footage. The list of screen shots should also include multiple camera angles, because lighting as well as background will affect the quality of the DV. Capturing images should be conducted with the video camera secured to a tripod. In some cases, the teacher will want to use a rolling tripod to capture a moving image.

Teachers should pay particular attention to the location of the subject within the frame. The subject should be located slightly off-center with plenty of "white space" between the subject and the frame. Zooming in too closely will eliminate white space. When a subject is in motion, white space is called "lead space," the area into which the subject (or the object that the subject is striking or kicking) will travel. The teacher must leave enough lead space in the frame so the subject does not travel out of the frame to complete the action. For example, if videotaping a student punting a football, the teacher should be sure to allow enough space inside the frame to capture the full extension of the leg as the foot contacts the football.

The *one-third rule* refers to how the subject picture is framed by the photographer in the viewing lens. It is a combination of white space and lead space in that it attempts to always capture the subject in the outer third of the frame, not the center. The majority of the subject may appear in the center, but parts of the subject may be in the outer third or even "bleeding" out of the picture. In figure 12.1, the one-third rule keeps the eyes of the audience always adjusting and focusing on the movement of the image across the frame. Student discontent and boredom sets in when the image remains stagnant and centered. This rule is of particular importance when capturing video for the purpose of telling stories.

Figure 12.1   The grid placed over the photo shows how the one-third rule applies.

DIGITAL VIDEO EDITING AND PRODUCTION

After the teacher has captured an ample supply of video footage, it is time to begin the process of editing. The best way to connect the computer for editing is through the use of an IEEE or firewire cable. These cables do not increase the speed of upload of the video to the computer but provide for better quality than RCA cables (yellow, red, and white). When a camera is turned on and the cable plugged into both the camera and the computer, the computer will automatically recognize the new hardware, requesting action from the user. Once the camera is recognized, the teacher should select the editing software (e.g., iMovie, Movie Maker, Movie Shaker) for importing the video. The imported video will be stored as a single clip or as several clips in the clip pane of the software. There is some debate as to whether the video should be uploaded in its entirety or in smaller clips. We recommend uploading only the quality video segments that will likely be included in the final product. The video loaded into the clip pane will be in a raw format, requiring large amounts of virtual memory; therefore, extra, unneeded video just takes up valuable memory space.

Regardless of the software package, once the video is imported into the clip panes (see figure 12.2) the editing process begins. Each video segment can be shortened by removing unwanted frames. Because the images were captured at 30 frames per second, the teacher can edit out a sneeze or any other distracting noise in the background by removing a few frames. The viewer will likely not even notice the missing frames because the human eye cannot see that many frames per second.

Once the teacher is satisfied with the length and quality of the video clips, it is time to drag the video clips onto the virtual storyboard. The teacher can view the clips from either the *Storyboard* view or the *Timeline* view. The timeline view includes audio as well as video to allow for synchronization. From the storyboard view, the teacher sequences the clips, places transitions between clips, adds titles, and adds text to the video (see figure 12.3). The more advanced the software is, the more a user can manipulate the video.

The teacher should continue to add media to the movie, stopping at each addition to preview the movie and examine the effects. The preview can be conducted in a small window or full screen; it is the user's choice. If satisfied with the appearance of the entire movie, the teacher then "renders" the file so it can be compressed and shared. This process usually takes a few minutes. Just prior to rendering, the teacher must select the movie format for the final product. For example, if the teacher wants to send a video through e-mail, the file will need to be small, thus resulting in a lower quality. If the final product is for use on a DVD player, then the movie may be saved as an MPEG4 or DVD-quality file. This decision was made by the teacher in the initial design phase prior to video capture, but it is revisited when the video needs to rendered and shared.

MULTIMEDIA INNOVATIONS

Quality physical education teachers seek ways to increase their students' engagement in physi-

Figure 12.2 Importing video.

Figure 12.3 Adding clips to the storyboard.

cal activity. The most effective strategies and innovations result in successful engagement by both high- and low-skilled students. Physical educators, however, sometimes struggle with the challenges of assessing student performance, providing feedback about motor skills, and managing the class.

A new innovation, the Virtual Gym, addresses the concerns of physical educators about providing age-appropriate practice and physical activity by simulating authentic game situations. Virtual Gym is a learning center that uses video technology to provide appropriate physical practice for all learners during physical education classes. As students physically interact with video images projected on the wall of the gymnasium, they are engaged in specific practice or assessment protocols. The protocols, designed by physical educators, are presented in real game situation contexts. For example, if the task requires throwing a football 10 yards, the image is projected on a wall at that same distance so that the performer must be able to complete the pass to the target 10 yards away. By observing the results of the skill attempt, the learner receives instant feedback (by personal observation, or peer feedback) about the success of the performance (knowledge of results).

Virtual Gym provides specific visual instructions for the motor task (e.g., three-step drop). After the learner replicates the task successfully, she moves on to the next level, which requires her to make decisions in a gamelike situation (e.g., as the quarterback, the learner performs a three-step drop, looks for an open receiver, and then throws a pass to the virtual image projected on the wall). Using a scoring rubric, a peer or teacher assesses whether the learner met the standard of competent performance.

The Virtual Gym provides students with the much-needed practice of skills in an appropriate range of contexts directly related to their level of development (skill and cognitive) while accommodating various learning styles (Rink, 2004). This innovation has been successfully integrated into many schools and resulted in increased student motivation and increased quality opportunities to respond (OTRs). It has also provided students with a choice of challenge levels (Fiorentino & Castelli, 2005b). Although innovations such as Virtual Gym have been successful, these virtual experiences should not replace physical practice in the actual game situations.

Multimedia innovations should be student centered and give students the opportunity to select their level of challenge. When used properly, multimedia innovations can enhance student decision making by placing them in a position to choose their physical response. For example, as the virtual quarterback in Virtual Gym, the student must decide which wide receiver is the best option. These innovations also allow students to take responsibility for their learning.

Multimedia innovations can help teachers assess students consistently. For example, teachers can have difficulty knowing how much students' performances may be affected by their peers' performances. Multimedia innovations can be designed to provide replicable, ideal assessments of gamelike situations.

SUMMARY

DV can make a contribution to teaching in physical education through the manipulation of video footage. True multimedia projects include text, video, and audio to foster student learning. These video productions can be shared through e-mail or for playback on DVD players, yet this should be determined by the teacher in the early stages of planning and development. Physical education students are receptive to new multimedia innovations such as Virtual Gym. Despite the successful integration of multimedia, virtual practice should not replace real teacher interactions and real practice experiences.

LEARNING MODULES

The learning modules are available to download from the companion Web site at www.HumanKinetics.com/PhysicalEducationTechnologyPlaybook.

Teacher Module 12.1   Digital Storytelling

The teacher modules in this chapter are designed to refine teachers' DV editing skills by requiring them to create digital biographies and virtual learning situations for their students. In the first teacher module, teachers use a variety of media to describe their personal and professional teaching philosophies. The digital story, including a personal teaching philosophy, is an ideal artifact for a professional portfolio.

Teacher Module 12.1
Digital Storytelling

Objective
To create a digital story using digital images to express your teaching philosophy.

National Standards for Beginning Physical Education Teachers
Standard 8 Reflection. Understand the importance of being a reflective practitioner and its contribution to overall professional development and actively seek opportunities to sustain professional growth.

Materials
*Computer workstations
*Digital video cameras
*Microphones
*Headphones (optional)
*Firewire cables
*Windows Movie Maker software (found on all computers using Windows 2000 or later)

Discussion Questions
*How can teachers use videotaping to facilitate learning, but still respect the rights of others?
*How can teachers maximize the effect of visual images to convey messages?
*What are the most important aspects to convey through visual media?
*What should be avoided in visual media productions?

Directions
Digital storytelling involves using images, music, narrative, and voice together to describe an individual's persona. In this module you will create a two- to three-minute digital video (DV) clip that is a first-person narrative, in your own voice, describing your teaching philosophy. This DV should reflect a professional image and should be included as an artifact in your portfolio.

1. Create a script of what you want to say in the video segment about your personality, teaching style, teaching philosophy, and teaching experiences.
2. Using a storyboard, identify scenes for which you could capture video. You may want to speak directly into the camera, or you may want to include a brief video of yourself giving directions to students.
3. Set up a video camera on a tripod. You can have a friend serve as the camera operator, or you can do the recording yourself.
4. Record more "takes" than you think you will need (after you watch the video, you will discover little things about the video that you will want to change). The intent of this video is not to do large amounts of editing, but simply to refine your awareness of critical factors related to DV capture and to improve your verbal and nonverbal communication skills.

Teacher Module 12.1 Digital Storytelling   1
From *Physical Education Technology Playbook* by Darla Castelli and Leah Holland Fiorentino, 2008, Champaign, IL: Human Kinetics.

Teacher Module 12.1   Digital Storytelling is available to download from the companion Web site.

Teacher Module 12.2   Virtual Gym

The second teacher module requires teachers to create virtual teaching and learning assessment centers for students. There are multiple reasons for elementary physical educators to consider creating virtual multimedia productions. Multimedia productions assist teachers in addressing a wide range of learning styles through the creation of meaningful, appropriate practice to improve skill acquisition. In addition, they provide successful conditions in which to increase student motivation, increase quality opportunities to respond (OTRs), and provide students with a choice of challenge levels. The production of multimedia should focus on student attainment of the National Association for Sport and Physical Education (NASPE) physical education standards (2004).

Teacher Module 12.2
Virtual Gym

Objective
To create a virtual teaching and learning assessment center for students.

National Standards for Beginning Physical Education Teachers
*Standard 6 Planning and Instruction. Understand the importance of planning developmentally appropriate instructional units to foster the development of a physically educated person.
*Standard 7 Student Assessment. Understand and use the varied types of assessment and their contribution to the overall program and the development of the physical, cognitive, social, and emotional domains.
*Standard 9 Technology. Use information technology to enhance learning and personal and professional productivity.

Materials
*Computer workstations
*Digital video cameras
*DVD/CD player or laptop
*LCD projector
*Extension cord

Discussion Questions
*How can teachers use videotaping to facilitate learning, but still respect the rights of others?
*What is virtual reality?
*How can virtual situations enhance student learning?

Directions
The process of taking video with the camera and then moving it from the camera to the computer is called *capture*. For this assignment, you will use video footage that depicts multiple attempts at motor skill performance in game-play situations. The footage should be carefully planned to reflect authentic situations that will appropriately challenge the students in your class.

Video Capture
No amount of editing can turn poor footage into an excellent digital video clip. The simple rule is: "Garbage in . . . garbage out."
1. Consider the age of participants and a media release.
    a. Obtain parental permission (if minors are involved).
    b. Use participants who are the same age as the target audience.
2. Consider the filming location.
    a. Use a natural background.
    b. Minimize distractions.
    c. A busy background has lots of colors and therefore uses large files.

Teacher Module 12.2 Virtual Gym   1
From *Physical Education Technology Playbook* by Darla Castelli and Leah Holland Fiorentino, 2008, Champaign, IL: Human Kinetics.

Teacher Module 12.2   Virtual Gym is available to download from the companion Web site.

Lesson Plan 12.1
Digital Storytelling
Grades 9-12

Objective
To create a digital story using digital images to display at least one responsible action in a physical activity setting.

National Standards for Physical Education
*Standard 5: Exhibits responsible personal and social behavior that respects self and others in physical activity settings.
*Standard 6: Values physical activity for health, enjoyment, challenge, self-expression, and/or social interaction.

Materials
*Computer workstations
*Digital video cameras
*Windows Movie Maker (found on all computers using Windows 2000 or later)

Accompanying Files
*LP12.1Student_Instructions
*LP12.1Worksheet (Storyboard)

Set Induction
What is social responsibility? How can we promote it in physical education or other physical activity settings? What is good sporting behavior? What is its importance in the physical activity setting? Digital storytelling requires that you use images, music, narrative, and voice together to describe your group's approach to socially responsible behaviors. You will create a one- to two-minute digital video (DV) clip promoting good sporting behavior and social responsibility in a physical activity setting.

Activity
1. You will need to impress upon the students that the planning part of the assignment is just as important as the capturing of the video. It is during the planning phase that the students identify what story they want to tell and how the message will be delivered.
2. The students should write their own scripts. If there will be multiple people in the video, each person's part should be written. At this step, the students will need to decide if they want the people in the video to actually say the words or if they want to read the text in a voice-over for the video.
3. Using the storyboard handout, the students will now draw what each video shot will look like. The storyboard is similar to a comic strip. Each box of the storyboard should contain the props, the actors, the camera angles, and the purpose of the shot.

Lesson Plan 12.1 Digital Storytelling   1
From *Physical Education Technology Playbook* by Darla Castelli and Leah Holland Fiorentino, 2008, Champaign, IL: Human Kinetics.

Lesson Plan 12.1 Digital Storytelling is available to download from the companion Web site.

Lesson Plan 12.2
Student-Created Virtual Gym
Grades 9-12

Objective
To create a Virtual Gym motor skill practice station for you and your friends to use to improve your performance on a specific sport task.

National Standards for Physical Education
*Standard 1: Demonstrates competency in motor skills and movement patterns needed to perform a variety of physical activities.
*Standard 2: Demonstrates understanding of movement concepts, principles, strategies, and tactics as they apply to the learning and performance of physical activities.

Materials
*Computer workstations
*Digital video cameras
*Firewire cables
*Microphones (optional)

Accompanying File
LP12.2Student_Instructions

Set Induction
Video images are a great way for you to view your motor skill from a different perspective. What kinds of sport skills do you do well? Which one of those skills would be important to capture on video and watch in slow motion? What is the importance of those skills in actual game-play situations?

Activity
1. Explain to the students that they will be working in small groups to create their own versions of Virtual Gym for their favorite sport activities.
2. This lesson can be integrated into a current unit or used as a final project for physical education. If you choose to integrate this assignment into a unit, you should help the students to identify all of the possible times during game play that an individual makes decisions. For example, a quarterback in a flag football unit must decide which receiver is open to receive a pass. You will want to work with the students to generate a list of acceptable motor movements that can be used for this project. The sky is the limit; as mentioned in chapter 12, you could create a Virtual Gym practice situation for any sport or situation such as goalkeeping in soccer; defending in lacrosse; blocking or spiking in volleyball; hitting a slow pitch softball; or performing a skateboard trick.
3. The students will need to make this sport skill as authentic as possible, so videotaping should take place in an appropriate facility using appropriate equipment.

Lesson Plan 12.2 Student-Created Virtual Gym   1
From *Physical Education Technology Playbook* by Darla Castelli and Leah Holland Fiorentino, 2008, Champaign, IL: Human Kinetics.

Lesson Plan 12.2 Student-Created Virtual Gym is available to download from the companion Web site.

Lesson Plan 12.1 Digital Storytelling

Both lesson plans in this chapter focus on students' skills in the capture and editing of DV. In the first lesson, students use digital storytelling strategies to share ideas about good sporting behavior and social responsibility in physical activity settings. Although the video is captured within the physical activity setting, we suggest that the digital editing take place outside of physical education class time.

Lesson Plan 12.2 Student-Created Virtual Gym

In the second lesson plan, students generate a virtual practice situation. The final products will ultimately promote physical activity, but the making of multimedia productions means dedicating some time to development in a non-physical-activity setting.

Physical Education Software

Laptops lined up in a single row on the stage at the far end of the gymnasium await the arrival of the students. They contain instructional software specific to physical education. Entering the gymnasium, the sixth-grade students are used to seeing this setup, because this is the fifth time this school year that you have integrated physical education–specific software into your lesson. You have posted the technology rules next to the physical education class guidelines, and as the students enter the gymnasium, you take a moment to remind the students that there are computers in the room today and they will be working with them at some of the stations. On the board is a list of students' names along with their assigned learning stations. Students find their names and spring into action, going to their specific learning stations and immediately beginning to work on various jump rope skills, routines, and fitness activities. The students at the laptops are identifying the muscles used during the jump rope skills, planning a physical activity program using jump ropes, and associating health-related fitness terms to jump rope activities. The room is abuzz as students move from station to station without direction from you. Students are engaged in the content, and you act as a facilitator.

Each of the technologies introduced to this point in this textbook was originally designed for business rather than educational settings. This chapter describes the integration of physical education–specific instructional software designed to enhance student comprehension of movement principles and concepts. Instructional software is different from productivity software in that it addresses student needs over those of the teacher. Additionally, this type of software is typically specific to a subject matter. Until the early 1990s, little instructional software existed, but today physical education teachers have many options for integrating software into their instructional plans. This chapter attempts to address NASPE teaching standards 2 (growth and development), 6 (planning and instruction), and 9 (technology) through the integration of physical education–specific software into the gymnasium.

The selection of instructional software is an important decision, but teachers can be overwhelmed by the catalogues, Web sites, and Internet host advertisements depicting all of the possibilities. Because funds are limited, physical education teachers must make purchases that will result in the greatest return. If they don't make their selections correctly the first time, they could waste the money they have. Teachers should also be aware that the selection and subsequent integration of software is a time-consuming and difficult process. Yet, evidence in mathematics and reading instruction suggests that instructional software improves student performance (Kulik, 1994).

USE OF INSTRUCTIONAL SOFTWARE

According to Bonnie Mohnsen (2008), teachers should consider four things prior to the selection and integration of instructional software: *(1)* the lesson objectives, *(2)* the teaching strategy, *(3)* the alignment of the instructional software with program goals and lesson objectives, and *(4)* the mechanism of integration. Many effective teachers begin planning by first identifying the national or state physical education standard that they want to address in the lesson. Implementing the standards in practice is not an easy task, because standards are merely stated expectations of what learners need to achieve; they are not activities or lesson plans in and of themselves. Therefore, the teacher must determine which activities are most likely to

result in students' learning the content addressed in the standard. Regardless of whether the lesson contains technology, the teacher should always begin planning with the standard in mind.

The learning objectives of a lesson provide a means for measuring student progress toward the attainment of national or state physical education standards. By identifying what students will be able to know, value, or do at the end of the lesson, the teacher can determine the most appropriate activities and the most effective activity sequence to facilitate attainment of the objectives. Instructional software can be included as an activity that supports the attainment of the learning objectives. As suggested in chapter 2, teachers who cannot positively respond to the following questions should question the need to integrate technology: *(1)* How will technology improve teacher efficiency? *(2)* How will the integration of technology foster learning? and *(3)* How does the technology accomplish something that previously could not be accomplished?

In the vignette for this chapter, students use Muscle Flash, Elementary Version 7, to name, locate, and determine the function of 29 muscles. The software program uses age-appropriate terms and definitions and video clips to illustrate muscle actions. The students in the vignette are required to identify which of the 29 muscles are used in various jump rope skills. At a second learning station the students view the Comprehensive Short Jump Rope CD, which is combined with the physical practice of various jump rope skills. This instructional software has five parts: an interactive learning section, portfolio, multiple choice quiz, task cards, and video clips for showing on handheld computers. Each of these applications is intended to facilitate the attainment of standards related to motor competence and the comprehension of movement concepts and principles.

TEACHING STRATEGY

Technology-using teachers employ a variety of teaching styles to integrate technology into the curriculum, especially the use of indirect, student-centered methods. The careful integration of instructional software allows students to work at their own pace, select their level of challenge, and establish an environment of collaborative learning. The novelty of the content and student experiences will influence the instructional strategies employed for a given lesson. Integration of instructional software is most effective when the software matches the teaching style. For example, some software programs focus on drill and practice with the students identifying, defining, and listing information that they recall from reading the materials included in the software. Other software programs are highly nonlinear and allow students to play the role of coach and develop practice plans for a team. The teacher should determine which strategy to use and then determine at which stage in the instructional unit the software would be best integrated.

ALIGNING INSTRUCTIONAL SOFTWARE WITH PROGRAM GOALS AND LESSON OBJECTIVES

The selection of instructional software and the timing of its integration are important factors. Many instructional software companies offer free demonstration copies or time-sensitive downloads over the Internet. Teachers should take advantage of these opportunities to evaluate the appropriateness of software prior to purchasing.

To adequately judge the potential for aligning the multimedia software with program and lesson goals, a teacher must judge the content; type and font; graphics, visuals, and sounds; and level of language. Each year the teacher will have already identified the content students will cover during the academic year through the written scope and sequence of the physical education curriculum. To determine the appropriateness of software programs, teachers should decide whether they align with their long-term plans.

The type and font of the instructional software can indicate whether the readability of the materials and the chunking of the information are appropriate for the students' learning level. The use of headers, italics, and bolding within the text serve as organizational markers to assist learners. When creating headings, sans serif fonts should be used, and serif fonts should be used for the body of the text. If the text contains too many of these features, students could be overwhelmed. If the text contains few or none of these features, students may become lost or confused. Teachers should pay close attention to type and font when evaluating instructional software.

Graphics, visuals, and sounds should be simplistic and supportive of navigation, not distracting.

Navigational buttons should be functional and highlighted by brief text to alert students to what will happen when they press them. Software programs containing teaching cues, tutorials, and help directories are more effective than those without these features. Moving graphics such as GIFs and the overuse of sound effects can reduce student motivation. During the evaluation, teachers should try all of the navigational buttons, imagining that they are the age of the students who will be using the software.

An instructional program whose Flesch reading level does not match students' reading level should not be used. Programs that can be accessed in both Spanish and English are preferred over those only in English. Although these features are often noted on the software packaging, teachers should confirm their existence through actual experimentation.

To adequately judge the potential for aligning the instructional software with program and lesson goals, teachers must also determine the function, pedagogical aspects, and technical aspects of the software. Instructional software serves many purposes, from drill and practice to problem solving. Teachers must determine whether the function of the software aligns with their lesson purposes. Some programs act only as tutorials for the self-teaching of content. More effective tutorials include some type of assessment of student learning, whereas simulations and problem-solving programs force students to use higher-order thinking skills with greater cognitive demands. Simulations tend to be more authentic and require students to make decisions within lifelike situations; this can be very effective in physical activity virtual environments.

Each software program can support various pedagogical foundations. Some programs provide timely, congruent feedback to the learner, but teachers should evaluate the frequency and appropriateness of that feedback. Specifically, some programs give feedback such as, "Sorry, your answer is incorrect; please try again." Programs that can be modified for various ability levels are more cost-effective than those that cannot. Teachers should note the amount of student choice the program offers and whether it promotes a collaborative learning environment. Once they have assessed the quality of a program, teachers must determine whether it aligns with the learning objectives.

The final teacher decision involves the technical aspects of the software. Software must be easy to use and navigate and free of glitches, and it must install smoothly onto computers. The availability of format (i.e., PC or Macintosh) may be a limiting factor, because not all software designed for PCs can be used on Macintosh computers and vice versa. However, third-party software such as Boot Camp can make it possible for Windows software to be used on Macintosh computers. Features such as help directories and tutorials are always useful.

INCORPORATING INSTRUCTIONAL SOFTWARE INTO PHYSICAL EDUCATION

Many teachers are willing to integrate physical education instructional software into lessons, yet they are concerned about the increase in sedentary time during physical education class. However, inactivity does not result from technology; rather, it is a by-product of poor planning on the part of the teacher. The presence of technology in the gymnasium should promote and lead to a better understanding of physical activity and thereby promote increased physical activity levels in the long run.

For the most effective integration strategy, we recommend using instructional software in four situations: *(1)* on days when the gymnasium is unavailable, *(2)* outside of physical education class during study hall or as a homework assignment, *(3)* in collaboration with classroom teachers as an interdisciplinary activity, or *(4)* as a learning station embedded in the lesson in the gymnasium in conjunction with physical practice. Successful integration requires careful planning, preparation, and practice of routines and protocols. Technology is effectively integrated when students are able to select technology tools to help them obtain information in a timely manner, analyze and synthesize the information, and present it professionally. The technology should be an integral part of the classroom and as accessible as all other classroom tools.

SUMMARY

With careful advanced planning, physical educators can successfully integrate instructional software into their classes. The level of success is determined by the alignment of the software with instructional goals and the means of incorporation within the unit. A critical phase is the evaluation of the instructional software. To determine the appropriateness of instructional software, teachers must judge the content; type and font; graphics, visuals, and sounds; and language. They must also evaluate the function, pedagogical aspects, and technical aspects of the software. Judging the appropriateness of an instructional software package is a complex process that takes time. Finally, if the selection of software is intended to increase physical activity, not decrease it, then the integration of the software into the curriculum should include plans to provide ample space, time, equipment, and teacher instruction to insure that students are, in fact, active.

LEARNING MODULES

The learning modules are available to download from the companion Web site at www.HumanKinetics.com/PhysicalEducationTechnology Playbook.

Teacher Module 13.1 Software Evaluation

The first teacher module in this chapter requires teachers to evaluate physical education–specific software. Teachers use the criteria described in this chapter to assess the relevance of specific instructional software.

> **Teacher Module 13.1**
> **Software Evaluation**
>
> **Objective**
> To evaluate instructional software using a worksheet.
>
> **National Standards for Beginning Physical Education Teachers**
> *Standard 6 Planning and Instruction. Understand the importance of planning developmentally appropriate instructional units to foster the development of a physically educated person.
> *Standard 9 Technology. Use information technology to enhance learning and personal and professional productivity.
>
> **Materials**
> *Computer workstations
> *Software (see list of software below or visit Bonnie's Fitware at http://www.pesoftware.com/demos.html to download a demonstration copy)
>
> **Accompanying File**
> TM13.1Worksheet (Software Evaluation)
>
> **Discussion Questions**
> *How can instructional software enhance learning?
> *What does the gymnasium look like when a teacher chooses to integrate instructional software into a lesson plan?
> *What should be done to eliminate the downtime often associated with technology integration?
>
> **Directions**
> 1. From the following list, select two instructional software packages to evaluate. If you do not have these on the computer that you are using, conduct a Web search to locate a free demonstration copy for your review.
> 2. Evaluate the software by completing the Software Evaluation worksheet (filename: TM13.1Worksheet). You will need to complete a worksheet for each of the software packages you evaluate.
>
> **General Instructional Software**
> *Virtual Exercise Physiology Lab
> *A.D.A.M.
> *Inspiration or Kidspiration
> *Software from the Learning Co.
> *Language Lab software
> *Chemistry or Physics Lab software
>
> Teacher Module 13.1 Software Evaluation   1
> From *Physical Education Technology Playbook* by Darla Castelli and Leah Holland Fiorentino, 2008, Champaign, IL: Human Kinetics.

Teacher Module 13.1 Software Evaluation is available to download from the companion Web site.

Teacher Module 13.2 Volleyball Complete

The second teacher module requires teachers to create a lesson plan that incorporates the use of Bonnie's Fitware Volleyball Complete for a volleyball unit at either the middle school or high school level. Enactment is the most difficult phase of integration. This module is ideal for use in a teaching field experience, because the lesson could be implemented and assessed for effectiveness.

> **Teacher Module 13.2**
> **Volleyball Complete**
>
> **Objective**
> To create a lesson plan that incorporates the use of physical education–specific software for a sport unit for either middle school or high school students.
>
> **National Standards for Beginning Physical Education Teachers**
> *Standard 6 Planning and Instruction. Understand the importance of planning developmentally appropriate instructional units to foster the development of a physically educated person.
> *Standard 9 Technology. Use information technology to enhance learning and personal and professional productivity.
>
> **Materials**
> *Computer workstations
> *Physical education–specific software
>
> **Discussion Questions**
> *How can a physical education teacher address the cognitive domain?
> *Are interactive software packages available for physical education teachers to use that stimulate students to think more deeply about a sport?
> *How can this technology be integrated into physical education classes?
>
> **Directions**
> 1. Conduct a Web search to identify possible physical education–specific software packages. This software should address sport participation, not simply health-related fitness content. (If you are looking for ideas for software, see TM 13.1.)
> 2. Once a title has been identified, download a trial or demonstration copy or order a copy of the software.
> 3. Prepare your computer by installing the software.
> 4. Familiarize yourself with all possible features of the software from the simplest to the most complex tasks.
> 5. Review all tasks that a K-12 student could complete using this software.
> 6. Identify the age appropriateness and readability of the content and determine how students would use this software.
> 7. Make a list of ways that you could integrate this software into a physical education lesson (e.g., use it as a learning center, bring the students to a lab setting, have the students design their own practice plans, and so on).
> 8. Align this software content with a desired learning outcome related to a NASPE physical education content standard.
>
> Teacher Module 13.2 Volleyball Complete   1
> From *Physical Education Technology Playbook* by Darla Castelli and Leah Holland Fiorentino, 2008, Champaign, IL: Human Kinetics.

Teacher Module 13.2 Volleyball Complete is available to download from the companion Web site.

Lesson Plan 13.1
Sim Athlete
Grades 9-12

Objective
To use the Sim Athlete software to create a practice or training schedule for an athlete.

National Standards for Physical Education
*Standard 1: Demonstrates competency in motor skills and movement patterns needed to perform a variety of physical activities.
*Standard 2: Demonstrates understanding of movement concepts, principles, strategies, and tactics as they apply to the learning and performance of physical activities.
*Standard 4: Achieves and maintains a health-enhancing level of physical fitness.

Materials
*Computer workstations
*Sim Athlete software (see Bonnie's Fitware at www.pesoftware.com)

Accompanying File
LP13.1Student_Instructions

Set Induction
You have a friend who has decided to try out for the school basketball team. Your friend has never really played basketball before but enjoys watching the game and wants to be part of a team. Because you are a current member of the basketball team, your friend asks you for help in preparing and training for the season, which starts in two months. What advice or help can you give your friend? What will your friend need to do to get ready for the season?

Activity
1. You will need to obtain a site license or download a demonstration copy of Sim Athlete from Bonnie's Fitware Web site.
2. We have enacted this lesson in the gym as well as in the computer lab. For the younger students, we used this software on one to three laptop learning stations set up on the stage located in the gym. Students physically practiced movement skills, such as dribbling and passing, for the basketball unit. They then rotated to the laptop station and planned practice for someone who had a goal of becoming a better basketball player. Aligning the physical practice with the cognitive practice planning helped the students to come to a better understanding of the concepts. The older students could go to a computer lab or complete this assignment outside of class, during a study hall or computer lab time.
3. Once the laptops have been set up with the desired software, you simply need to distribute the student instructions. You can have the students work independently or in pairs. Working in partners always helps with troubleshooting because two students can attempt to solve the problems by themselves first and then contact you, if needed.

Lesson Plan 13.1 Sim Athlete   1
From *Physical Education Technology Playbook* by Darla Castelli and Leah Holland Fiorentino, 2008, Champaign, IL: Human Kinetics.

Lesson Plan 13.1 Sim Athlete is available to download from the companion Web site.

Lesson Plan 13.1 Sim Athlete

These lesson plans provide the students with an opportunity to use physical education–specific software. The first lesson requires the use of Sim Athlete (Bonnie's Fitware Inc.) to create a practice or training schedule for an athlete. Drawing on students' previous knowledge, this software simulates a coaching situation in which the coach must design practice plans for the players. The index in the software could also serve as a reference for definitions of key concepts used in physical education curricula.

Lesson Plan 13.2
Health-Related Fitness
Grades 6-8

Objective
To work with a group to present information to the class about a particular fitness component.

National Standards for Physical Education
Standard 2: Demonstrates understanding of movement concepts, principles, strategies, and tactics as they apply to the learning and performance of physical activities.

Materials
*Computer workstations
*Health-Related Fitness software (see Bonnie's Fitware at www.pesoftware.com)

Accompanying File
LP13.2Student_Instructions

Set Induction
When people say they are "in shape," what does that mean? How do you know whether and when you are physically fit? You will be learning about five components of physical fitness and assessing your own health using the Health-Related Fitness software from Bonnie's Fitware.

Activity
1. Make sure you are familiar with the software before using it in your class.
2. Students will need to have completed the Fitnessgram/Activitygram test and have access to the class (not individual student) scores for each part.
3. Divide the students into small groups and assign them a specific laptop or computer station.
4. Each group will also be assigned to review a specific health-related fitness component (cardiorespiratory endurance, flexibility, muscular strength, muscular endurance, or body composition). Briefly review the definitions of these terms with the students; however, remember that one student will be assigned to use the *Concepts* part of the software to define the health-related fitness terms.
5. Each group should have one student take on each of these responsibilities:
    a. *Assess* the student performance on the specific health-related fitness program.
    b. If the students have not yet completed the Fitnessgram test, *Format* the fitness tests that the student would have to complete.
    c. Select *Exercises* that will help the students improve a specific health-related fitness concept.
    d. Type a summary that contains a definition of the health component and the exercises that will help to improve that health-related fitness concept.

Lesson Plan 13.2 Health-Related Fitness   1
From *Physical Education Technology Playbook* by Darla Castelli and Leah Holland Fiorentino, 2008, Champaign, IL: Human Kinetics.

Lesson Plan 13.2 Health-Related Fitness is available to download from the companion Web site.

Lesson Plan 13.2 Health-Related Fitness

The second lesson requires students to work in groups and to use Health-Related Fitness (Bonnie's Fitware Inc.) to create class presentations about a particular fitness component. Each group presents on a different fitness component and provides ample information, appropriate demonstrations, and authentic assessments of the class.

Technology in the Palm of Your Hand

Thirty-five personal digital assistants (PDAs) are in a carrying case on the table at the front of the gymnasium. As students finish their warm-up activity, they come to the table to pick up a PDA. Some students view their workout for the weight training instructional unit, while others take a quick quiz on the tactics of indoor soccer. When each student finishes with the PDA, the information is sent through an infrared beam back to the laptop computer stationed on the same table as the PDAs. Each upload of information takes only a few seconds, and the students quickly transition to the next activity. Later, as the lesson ends, you inform the students that they will be beginning a dance unit on Monday. During this unit, you would like the students to work in groups to create a dance routine. You further explain that the students will be using the PDAs and a software program called Sketchy to plan the routine. Each group will have a choreographer, technical adviser, custom designer, and dancer. The student in the role of technical adviser will oversee the use of the PDA as well as provide the music.

Since 1993, when Apple unveiled the Newton Message Pad, personal digital assistants (PDAs) have been used in the educational setting. It was estimated that over 17 million PDAs were purchased in 2007. A PDA is a handheld computer that was originally designed as a personal organizer containing basic features such as an address book, memo pad, and date book. Initially, issues such as memory and connectivity were limitations to usage and integration. Unlike a computer, a PDA frequently requires the use of a stylus rather than a keyboard to input information, although portable and virtual keyboards are available to enter data into PDAs. Advances in technology have now provided an option on some PDAs for voice and handwriting recognition for data input. This chapter attempts to address NASPE teaching standards 2 (growth and development) and 7 (student assessment) through data entry and the use of PDAs.

The primary attraction of PDAs is their low cost (around $100) and mobility, which make them functional in a variety of environments. With the advent of more efficient synchronization mechanisms such as beaming (an infrared exchange between PDAs and computers) and touch-sensitive screens, information can be synchronized with a laptop or computer rapidly. Advances in software have allowed Microsoft documents such as those generated in Word or Excel to be part of the information exchange. A teacher can create a lesson plan in Microsoft Word; then transfer the document to a PDA for reference while out on the playing field or on the deck of the pool. A more traditional transfer of information is called "HotSyncing"; this involves placing the PDA in a cradle connected to a computer to exchange information. Although this exchange is not as instantaneous as beaming, HotSyncing often results in fewer communication errors and a more efficient use of time, because the PDA batteries are being charged while it is stationed in the cradle.

In 2007, over 10,000 software programs were available for use in handheld computers. These programs include database managers, word processors, Web browsers, spreadsheets, and educational software. Much of this software is in the form of freeware and shareware and can be downloaded from the Internet. The amount of software available depends on the platform of the PDA. Handheld PDAs come in two formats: Palm OS and PocketPC. The major difference between the two is that the PocketPC uses a Windows Mobile operating system and performs much like a computer. Applications for the Palm OS platform will not work on PocketPC platforms and vice versa. This chapter focuses on the use and integration of Palm OS platform handheld devices.

POSSIBILITIES FOR PDAS

Many PDAs are capable of executing tasks similar to those executed by other handheld devices such as cell phones, MP3 players, and text messaging devices. Before purchasing a PDA or multiple PDAs for use in physical education programs, teachers should identify their essential features to ensure that they will meet the needs of the students. As with all technologies, the physical education teacher should compare models and prices and review the features of each PDA on a number of Web sites. The first step, of course, is clearly defining the purpose for the integration of the PDA into the physical education setting. Does the teacher need one PDA for instructional purposes or 30 PDAs for students to use individually?

When considering purchasing a PDA, teachers must consider *(1)* weight, *(2)* the importance of Bluetooth or Wi-Fi capabilities, *(3)* connectivity, *(4)* expandability, *(5)* the primary method of data input, and *(6)* multimedia applications. Weight is an important consideration. One rationale for integrating this device into the physical education program is to make life easier for the teacher; PDAs that are heavy, bulky, and cumbersome will not fit the bill. The Internet can help teachers compare models; however, we also recommend that teachers place the PDA in their hands before purchasing.

Wireless capabilities may not be a particularly important consideration for physical education teachers. Teachers who want to communicate wirelessly from the field should consider the cost of monthly service charges; fees can add up quickly. Despite the move of many schools to go wireless, the signals are usually not strong enough to extend beyond the gymnasium. To make an appropriate decision, the teacher should consult the media specialist or another technical assistant who understands the school's wireless capabilities.

Most PDAs come with a docking cradle to use for battery recharging and HotSyncing. It is important to ensure that the PDA will have seamless connectivity with the associated desktop or laptop computer. For example, some PDAs come with software that is best aligned with the e-mail program Microsoft Outlook, whereas others are more compatible with other software. Synchronization with e-mail is a feature that would be beyond the instructional benefits for physical education, yet may improve teacher efficiency.

Expandability can be an issue if the physical education teacher wishes to use the PDA for multiple purposes. For example, the teacher may use the address book for professional contacts, use the lesson plan software, take digital images, and enter student performance data. Because all of these functions require memory and storage space, a teacher looking to use them all should purchase a PDA that has an expansion slot. This allows the teacher to purchase a larger memory stick for additional storage space. Even inexpensive PDAs come with these features, but the teacher must determine which ones will be needed. Expandability is important for the investment to last more than a single academic year.

Teachers must consider how they will collect data and temporarily store them on the PDA. Choices include typing, tapping, or beaming information into the PDA. With the high efficiency of the synchronization, teachers can generate materials such as spreadsheets and scoring rubrics on a computer and move them to a PDA. Teacher must reflect on their preferences for entering data. Some like using a small collapsible keyboard, whereas others find this uncomfortable and prefer writing on the PDA itself. Writing recognition programs such as Pen Reader and Graffiti are readily available.

PDAs can also be used to capture digital images. However, aside from capturing unique moments when a camera is not available, we recommend using other devices for capturing images (see chapter 10). Because of storage space issues, images captured on PDAs are often small, have low resolution, and are of poor quality. Multimedia functionality should not be a primary determining factor in the purchase of a PDA. A teacher who already owns a digital camera should not buy a PDA with this feature. If the PDA will be used for capturing images, it should include an expansion slot, because more memory will be needed.

We recommend two brand of PDAs for physical education teachers, Palm Zire and PalmOne TX. Both are highly rated and have the ability to update and share Word, Excel, and PowerPoint files while on the go. The PalmOne TX has Wi-Fi and Bluetooth capabilities as well as multimedia features, thus increasing the price for features that a physical education program may not need. For personal use, we recommend the PalmOne TX. For professional use, the Palm Zire would be more appropriate.

PDAS IN EDUCATION

The use of handheld computers (PDAs) enhances student achievement (Soloway & Norris, 2006). According to the K12 Handheld organization (www.k12handheld.com), there are 101 reasons for an educator to consider the integration of handheld devices into the educational setting, one of which is enhancing student learning. Following are others:

- ► Tracking student progress toward attainment of standards
- ► Conducting authentic assessments
- ► Instantly accessing student information
- ► Recording grades
- ► Keeping inventories of equipment
- ► Accessing lesson plans
- ► Using rubrics to assess student work
- ► Tracking progress toward the attainment of fitness records

PDAs are easy to use, portable, and cost-effective and can share information rapidly.

The ability to track student performance and conduct authentic assessments is of particular importance to physical educators. Many physical education classes take place in a gymnasium, on a track, in a pool, or on a ball field. Teachers have traditionally used a clipboard, paper, and pencil to collect student assessment data. In this age of technology-enriched learning environments, teachers can type data into spreadsheets and analyze them before sharing them with students, parents, or administrators. They will also likely have to transfer the data into a gradebook software program for inclusion on a report card. With the use of the Documents To Go software program, a teacher can use a PDA to collect, store, interpret, and grade student performances. After mastery of the software, this system is far more efficient than the traditional method of collecting student performance data.

PDAs can also help to motivate and foster learning among the students. A PDA gives a teacher constant access to students' current grades, allowing them to show students their grades or performance levels at any time. Such immediate feedback can move students toward higher achievement and the mastery of specific tasks, enhancing their learning.

Students can also use PDAs. Software programs such as Sketchy, Cooties, and Idea Pad use PDAs to advance learning of particular concepts (Curtis, Williams, Norris, O'Leary & Soloway, 2003). Sketchy, created at the University of Michigan, is like the Paint application on most computers. Students can draw on the screen using the stylus and then apply text and color to the drawings. These drawings stimulate higher-order thinking and problem solving. Students can draw images of different balances or stunts that could be used in a gymnastics routine. From these images they can identify the center of gravity. The application of Sketchy is only limited by the imagination.

Cooties helps younger students understand that the transfer of germs is unhealthy. In Cooties, students have their own PDAs and walk around the room beaming a fun name into the PDAs of other students. This exchange of information simulates a handshake. The more people that someone shakes hands with, the more likely that person is to become ill. The image on the PDA for some students will depict them "becoming ill." These students learn the importance of hand washing, healthy eating, and physical activity in maintaining a healthy lifestyle.

Idea Pad is similar to the software program Inspiration in that it allows students to create concept maps. Idea Pad lets students draw diagrams, mind maps, or concept maps or create flow charts. This software even allows students to add text to the diagrams. Whether in kindergarten or college, students sometimes struggle to organize their thoughts and prioritize their actions. This application can help with both, because students are required to make healthy choices, reorganize their time to participate in more physical activity, or even contemplate healthy choices. Free downloads of other software programs are available at www.k12handhelds.com/freedownloads.php.

PDAs can disseminate workout information and help students record their performances during workouts. Because PDAs can be updated so quickly and contain multiple accounts of student information, 30 PDAs could help over 500 students log their physical activity or weight training programs. As discussed in the vignette at the beginning of the chapter, students can use PDAs during physical education class to determine what lifting exercise they should do as well as to record how many reps and sets they performed and the amount of weight they lifted. This information could be synced back to a computer for storage in a student or class portfolio. Once on the laptop, reports of student progress can be printed and distributed as progress reports or parental reports.

SUMMARY

PDAs can improve teacher efficiency and student learning. The Palm OS platform enables swift transfer of information from the desktop to the field and back again, thus improving information access. PDAs often have multiple functions and many features. Deciding which model to purchase can be difficult. We suggest using the K12 Handheld organization's list of 101 Educational Uses for Your Handheld to identify ways PDAs can be used in physical education. The number of applications available for the Palm OS platform is expanding daily. Authentic assessment and tracking of student progress are the most important applications of these technologies.

LEARNING MODULES

The learning modules are available to download from the companion Web site at www.HumanKinetics.com/PhysicalEducationTechnologyPlaybook.

Teacher Module 14.1   Documents To Go: Storing Observational Data

The teacher modules in this chapter require the use of a PDA to collect performance data. In the first teacher module, teachers use Documents To Go to create scoring rubrics using Microsoft Word and a spreadsheet using Microsoft Excel. These documents are then transferred to the PDA for data collection in the field. These data, once collected, are synced back to the computer for analysis and interpretation. (Without interpreting and eventually sharing this interpretation with the learner, little is gained, because feedback to the learner, not simply record keeping, is of the highest importance.)

> ### Teacher Module 14.1
> #### Documents To Go: Storing Observational Data
>
> **Objective**
> To create a student assessment scoring rubric, collect student performance data using a PDA, generate a student performance report, and design a lesson plan to meet the needs of the students, based on the assessment report.
>
> **National Standards for Beginning Physical Education Teachers**
> **Standard 7 Student Assessment.** Understand and use the varied types of assessment and their contribution to the overall program and the development of the physical, cognitive, social, and emotional domains.
>
> **Materials**
> *Computer workstations
> *PDAs
> *HotSync interfaces
> *Documents To Go Software (sometimes this is already on the PDAs)
>
> **Accompanying Files**
> *TM14.1Worksheet1 (Daily Behavior Rating for Physical Education)
> *TM14.1Worksheet2 (Daily Behavior Rating for Physical Education [Excel])
> *TM14.1Worksheet3 (High School Soccer Rubric [Excel])
> *TM14.1Worksheet4 (High School Soccer Rubric [Excel])
>
> **Discussion Questions**
> *What standards of performance are acceptable for students?
> *How can teachers effectively integrate student performance into their lesson plans?
>
> **Directions**
> 1. Set up your PDA.
>   a. To configure your PDA to operate with your computer, follow the instructions given by the materials that came with your PDA.
>   b. Be sure to confirm that the Documents To Go software has been installed on both your computer and the PDA.
>   c. Once the PDA has been configured for use, follow the next steps to create your assessment rubric.
> 2. Design a scoring rubric in Word.
>   a. A rubric is a rating scale that discriminates levels of performance among participants.
>   b. A rubric that awards everyone an A or 100% has been inappropriately designed. See worksheet 1 (filename: TM14.1Worksheet1) for an example of an effective rubric.
>   c. Identify the task to be rated. This can be a single task (free throw), a sequence of tasks (travel, roll, balance), or a rubric of game play (6v6 soccer).
>
> Teacher Module 14.1 Documents To Go: Storing Observational Data   1
> From *Physical Education Technology Playbook* by Darla Castelli and Leah Holland Fiorentino, 2008, Champaign, IL: Human Kinetics.

Teacher Module 14.1   Documents To Go: Storing Observational Data is available to download from the companion Web site.

Teacher Module 14.2   Teacher Observational Systems

The second teacher module has teachers collect time-related observational data using the GoObserve software program. This software allows teachers to evaluate personal teaching performances by tracking how they use their time during a lesson through self-identification or observation by another. Teachers who truly want to increase the amount of physical activity time within physical education class must be sensitive to the use of time. GoObserve records the frequency of observed teacher and student behaviors. The specific criteria can be customized so the teacher or administrator can focus on a specific behavior.

> ### Teacher Module 14.2
> #### Teacher Observational Systems
>
> **Objective**
> To use the PDA program GoObserve 1.0 to evaluate a teaching performance and generate a report.
>
> **National Standards for Beginning Physical Education Teachers**
> **Standard 9 Technology.** Use information technology to enhance learning and personal and professional productivity.
>
> **Equipment**
> *Computer workstations
> *PDAs
> *HotSync interfaces
> *GoObserve 1.0
>
> **Discussion Questions**
> *How can technology be used to give constructive feedback?
> *What are the advantages to using a PDA for observation and evaluation as opposed to pencil and paper?
>
> **Directions**
> 1. Launch GoObserve. From the Palm OS Launcher (you get to the launcher by selecting the circle with a picture of a house near the lower left corner of the screen), select the GoObserve icon. The icon looks like a magnifying glass with an A+ in it.
> 2. Select a teacher.
>   a. On the first screen of GoObserve, select the teacher to observe. You should see the list of teachers that you entered in the GoObserve desktop (on your PC).
>   b. If there are more teachers loaded than will fit on a single screen, a scroll bar appears on the right side of the screen. Use your stylus to move the list up and down to find the teacher, or use the physical up and down scroll buttons on the frame of the PDA.
>   c. Select the teacher being observed.
>   d. Now that you have highlighted a teacher, select the *Choose* button. This will take you to the *Criteria* screen (see figure 14.1).
> 3. Select *Criteria and Choosing Activities*.
>   a. The *Criteria* screen is used to help frame the observation goals. Select one or more criteria, then select *Begin*. This will take you to the *Activities* screen.
>   b. The *Activities* screen is where information is entered during the observation. Select one of the activities to start the observation (see figure 14.2).
>   c. Select the activity that most closely matches what is going on in the classroom at that time. As you see things happening that are noteworthy, enter them in the text field.
>   d. Save the entry by selecting *Enter*. This allows you to make a time-stamped note.
>
> Teacher Module 14.2 Teacher Observational Systems   1
> From *Physical Education Technology Playbook* by Darla Castelli and Leah Holland Fiorentino, 2008, Champaign, IL: Human Kinetics.

Teacher Module 14.2   Teacher Observational Systems is available to download from the companion Web site.

Lesson Plan 14.1
Cooties
Grades 4-6

Objective
To use the PDA program Cooties to learn about contracting a virus and then engage in a discussion of how viruses and diseases are spread and how virus contraction can be prevented.

National Standards for Physical Education
Standard 4: Achieves and maintains a health-enhancing level of physical fitness.

Materials
*Personal Digital Assistant (PDA) using the Palm OS platform (at least one for every two students)
*Cooties software (www.goknow.com/Products/Cooties)

Accompanying File
LP14.1Student_Instructions

Set Induction
Sometimes you can see that someone is ill; what does a sick person look like? Is it possible to be sick, yet look healthy? How can that be? What are some ways we can stay healthy even when we are around someone who is sick? Is everyone who is sick able to make you sick?

Activity
1. Make sure there are enough PDAs for the students (one per pair of students would be ideal).
2. Make sure the Cooties software is on each PDA.
3. Adjust the Cooties game parameters in the Teacher mode. You must select one of the PDAs as the person who will be infected and begin the spread of germs.
4. Each coodle (the character in the Cooties software) needs to have a unique name. Have the students make up a unique name. Do not have them use their own name because you do not want anyone being singled out as the person who spread the disease. This is a simulation game; we are not really spreading germs here.
5. This lesson works best if each pair of students can have a PDA; however, if more students need to share, have them choose one name for their coodle.
6. Begin the game by having students walk around the room and greet each other by infrared beaming their coodle names to one another's PDA. You may need to encourage the students to greet people other than their friends. If they are working in pairs, encourage them to take turns.
7. As the game continues, some coodles will start to appear ill by withering and shriveling. This represents poor health.
8. The coodles that become sick need to retrace their steps to see who they met who might have been sick. In some cases, it might have been as many as four or five people ago.

Lesson Plan 14.1 Cooties
From *Physical Education Technology Playbook* by Darla Castelli and Leah Holland Fiorentino, 2008, Champaign, IL: Human Kinetics.

Lesson Plan 14.1 Cooties is available to download from the companion Web site.

Lesson Plan 14.1 Cooties

The lesson plan allows students to use handheld devices to enhancing their own learning. Cooties facilitates learning about how viruses are contracted and diseases are spread. The purpose of the application and the integration of this technology is to provide a more student-centered approach to teaching the content.

Lesson Plan 14.2
Sketchy
Grades 6-8

Objectives
To use the Sketchy PDA software to draw a sequence of dance steps that will be played as a movie on the PDA, watched by others, and then practiced.

National Standards for Physical Education
*Standard 1: Demonstrates competency in motor skills and movement patterns needed to perform a variety of physical activities.
*Standard 2: Demonstrates understanding of movement concepts, principles, strategies, and tactics as they apply to the learning and performance of physical activities.

Materials
*Personal Digital Assistants (PDAs) containing Palm OS platform software (one for every two or three students)
*Sketchy software (www.goknow.com/Products/Sketchy/)

Accompanying File
LP14.2Student_Instructions

Set Induction
Drawings can help you to see things differently, but how can drawing help you to solve problems? What types of problems can be solved by drawing in a physical activity setting?

Activity
1. Sketchy was originally designed for use in science education; students used PDAs to draw cell structures observed under a microscope. Since that time, Sketchy has also been used to write and share stories or, in this case, to create a new dance.
2. You will need to go to the Go Know Web site and download the free demonstration software for use for educational purposes for 45 days or actually purchase a license for use of this product.
3. Once Sketchy is downloaded and placed on all of your PDAs, review how to use it. Make sure there is at least one PDA for every two or three students.
4. Have the Sketchy program already open on the PDAs when students receive them. Explain how to use it and your expectations.
5. Have different music selections for them to choose from.
6. Have each group discuss different dance steps or moves that they could use to this music.

Lesson Plan 14.2 Sketchy
From *Physical Education Technology Playbook* by Darla Castelli and Leah Holland Fiorentino, 2008, Champaign, IL: Human Kinetics.

Lesson Plan 14.2 Sketchy is available to download from the companion Web site.

Lesson Plan 14.2 Sketchy

This lesson helps a group of students to create a sequence of dance steps. Using a PDA, they draw pictures on the screen across a series of frames. After all the steps in the dance have been drawn on the PDA, the students can animate the drawings to see what their dance will look like. This learning tool is valuable for learners transitioning from rational to abstract learning.

Technology as a Measure of Physical Activity

Students enter the gymnasium holding their heart rate monitor straps, which have been purchased as part of the laboratory fees for physical education class. Polar heart rate monitor class management packs are hanging from the bleachers as the students enter. Each student finds the assigned heart rate monitor by number and quickly puts it on. An assigned student leads peers through a series of stretches after each student has completed a self-selected number of laps around the gymnasium. After you have taken attendance, you point out the team assignments on the wall and announce the field number that each team will be playing on. Because you have an odd number of teams, one team participates in Frisbee golf while the other four teams participate in two games of Ultimate Frisbee. The students are not competing for team supremacy in Frisbee, but taking part in a health-related fitness challenge. The team that spends the most physical education time in their target heart rate zone will get to choose the unit of instruction (pickleball or team building) for next week's physical education classes. Knowing this, many students choose to run, as opposed to walk, from hole to hole in Frisbee golf. The teams rotate through each field and the Frisbee golf course. As the class period comes to a close, the students remove their heart rate monitors and beam the data into a laptop computer located near the locker rooms. The electronic student physical activity logs are packed with daily step counts, the amount of time in the target heart zone, and evidence of reduced heart rate recovery time after physical activity. You review the data and determine which team spent the most time in the target heart zone.

Physical activity "is defined as bodily movement that is produced by the contraction of skeletal muscle and that substantially increases energy expenditure" (American College of Sports Medicine [ACSM], 2006, p. 3). Addressing issues related to physical inactivity among our youth has become a national health objective, because the incidence of obesity and type II diabetes has increased at alarming rates. Although one study (Trost et al., 2002) demonstrated that children exceed the minimum standard of activity as defined by the President's Council on Physical Fitness and Sports, it is estimated that nearly half of young people ages 12 to 21 are not vigorously active on a regular basis. Questionnaire data suggest that 20 to 50% of teenagers receive insufficient physical activity and that 6 to 12% do not perform any moderate or vigorous activity (Corbin, Pangrazi & Le Masurier, 2004). Given the present obesity epidemic and related explosion in type II diabetes, it is reasonable to consider physical education as "uniquely positioned to contribute across genders and socioeconomic levels to the solution" (Rink & Mitchell, 2003, p. 471). This chapter attempts to address NASPE teaching standards 2 (growth and development), 3 (diverse learners), and 6 (planning and instruction) through the use of pedometers and heart rate monitors.

To advance national wellness goals through the public school curricula, the Child Nutrition and WIC Act was reauthorized in 2004, requiring each school in the United States that participates in the School Lunch Act or the Child Nutrition Act programs to establish a comprehensive wellness policy to specifically address healthy eating and physical activity. The physical education teacher is encouraged to be part of the development and enactment of these policies. Including physical educators in the development of these policies at their own school helps to highlight the benefits of engaging children in physical activity beyond physical education classes.

Being physically active has many physical and mental benefits. Among the physical benefits are normal body weight, reduced risk for metabolic syndrome, improved bone health, and enhanced muscular strength and endurance. Academic achievement and faster, more accurate cognitive responses are positively related to aerobic fitness (Castelli, Hillman, Buck & Erwin, 2007). Despite these benefits, some physical education classes offer students minimal engagement in physical activity. For example, one study found that students spent an average of only 19 minutes engaged in moderate to vigorous physical activity during a 55-minute physical education class period (Coe, Pivarink, Womack, Reeves & Malina, 2006). The integration of technology can assist in the engagement of physical activity both during and beyond physical education.

Steps, calories, distance, heart rate, time in the target heart zone, and METs (1 MET representing resting metabolism) are all *measurable* physical activity outcomes that can be measured by pedometers or heart rate monitors. The integration of these technologies into the physical education curriculum can help teachers understand student differences. Physical education teachers cannot rely on traditional teaching practices and informal testing to monitor student progress toward achieving the national standards related to physical activity and fitness.

The President's Council on Physical Fitness and Sports recommends that children accumulate a minimum of 60 minutes (and up to several hours) of physical activity each day (Corbin, Pangrazi & Le Masurier, 2004). Tracking heart rate data and steps taken are two ways to integrate physical activity technologies, such as pedometers and heart rate monitors, into the curriculum to address the specific health needs of each student. Without these devices, it is difficult to determine whether a student is working at an appropriate intensity.

TECHNOLOGY AND HEALTH-RELATED FITNESS

Physical fitness is defined as a trait or a given set of attributes that a person possesses that are reciprocally related to physical activity (ACSM, 2006). More specifically, health-related physical fitness is associated with an ability to engage in daily activities with vitality and includes the components of aerobic capacity, muscle fitness, and body composition. Physical education curriculum content should address these health-related fitness concepts. Research findings have shown that to become physically fit and have positive attitudes toward fitness, people must understand (i.e., learn and apply) the concepts and principles of health-related fitness. Health-related fitness knowledge is positively related to physical activity levels (Kulinna & Silverman, 2000), and participation in physical education can help students meet their health-related fitness goals (i.e., increased physical activity) and improve health-related fitness knowledge (Hopper, Munoz, Gruber & Nguyen,

TABLE 15.1 Methods of Describing Physical Activity

Method	Description
Pedometers	When clipped to the waistband, pedometers use spring-loaded mechanisms to measure the up-and-down motion of the hips.
Direct observation	Trained observers follow participants for the entire measurement period time-sampling physical activity. Time-sampling involves documenting physical activity for a specific period (e.g., 1 minute) followed by a short break (e.g., 20 seconds).
Self-report	Participants document their activity level at the same time each day. Each morning they log their activity for the previous day. Some instruments collect data for two days; others collect for as many as seven days.
Heart rate monitors	Heart rate monitors indirectly assess physical activity by measuring the heart's response to physical activity. Heart rate increases with increases in the intensity of physical activity.
Uniaxial accelerometers	Uniaxial accelerometers generally measure body movement (usually at the hips) in the vertical plane. This movement is best thought of as an up-and-down motion. They are much more costly and larger than pedometers. They can record and print a record of all movements by the time of day.
Triaxial accelerometers	Triaxial accelerometers assess physical activity by measuring movement in three planes: side to side, vertical, and horizontal.

Reprinted, by permission, from A. Beighle, R.P. Pangrazi and S.D. Vincent, 2001, "Pedometers, physical activity, and accountability," *JOPERD* 72(9): 18.

2005). As students begin to apply health-related fitness concepts to their lives (Dale & Corbin, 2000), physical activity beyond that experienced during physical education class increases (Kulinna & Silverman, 2000).

One purpose of teaching health-related fitness content during physical education is to promote positive physical activity decision making during leisure time. As such, this education should expose students to a wide variety of activities that can enrich the quality of life as well as reduce the risk of coronary heart disease. This content also will help students understand how they can measure and track their own physical activity. This investment helps in both the short and long term because there is increasing evidence that trends of physical inactivity in adolescence continue into adulthood (Gordon-Larsen, Nelson & Popkin, 2004).

Many methods can be used to measure physical activity (see table 15.1). Although all of these methods are to some degree valid and reliable, objectivity varies. The most objective method, the accelerometer, is the most costly and therefore is most often used in research, not physical education, settings. Self-reports are subjective, because people must give meaning to their own physical activity by making comparisons to a standard.

Each of these methods has advantages and disadvantages. The most pragmatic tools are pedometers and heart rate monitors. The intent of this chapter is to introduce these technologies, increase teachers' level of comfort with them, and encourage participation in the initial phase of integration. To advance the integration of pedometers beyond a single event to one of more consistency and regularity, we recommend the book *Pedometer Power* by Pangrazi, Beighle, and Sidman, which provides a plan for integrating pedometers that is comprehensive and doable. For the integration of heart rate monitors, we recommend the textbook *Lessons From the Heart*, by Kirkpatrick. More information about these books can be found in the References and Resources.

SUMMARY

Today's youth need to learn to measure their physical activity. This assessment skill needs to be taught during physical education and supported outside of these classes. There is mounting evidence that health-related fitness knowledge is enhanced when technologies such as pedometers and heart rate monitors are integrated into physical education. Increased health-related fitness knowledge in turn increases students' engagement in physical activity. The teacher and student learning modules address how technology can initially be integrated into physical education lessons.

LEARNING MODULES

The learning modules are available to download from the companion Web site at www.HumanKinetics.com/PhysicalEducationTechnologyPlaybook.

Teacher Module 15.1
Pedometers

Objective
To design a physical activity program as part of a school wellness policy.

National Standards for Beginning Physical Education Teachers
Standard 2 Growth and Development. Understand how individuals learn and develop, and provide opportunities that support physical, cognitive, social, and emotional development.
Standard 6 Planning and Instruction. Understand the importance of planning developmentally appropriate instructional units to foster the development of a physically educated person.
Standard 10 Collaboration. Understand the necessity of fostering collaborative relationships with colleagues, parents/guardians, and community agencies to support the development of a physically educated person.

Materials
*Computer workstations
*Pedometers

Discussion Questions
*How can technology enhance and promote physical activity among students and the community?
*What is the Child Nutrition and WIC Reauthorization Act of 2004?

Directions
Teachers are required to integrate pedometers in the context of the Child Nutrition and WIC Reauthorization Act of 2004. It is important for a teacher to use a pedometer because modeling the desired outcome of regular physical activity by the teacher increases the likelihood of student engagement.

1. You will be assigned a pedometer to wear for a two-week period.
2. Clip the pedometer to the waistline of your pants or shorts on the right side of your body, in line with the midline of your leg.
3. Press the reset button after clipping on the pedometer.
4. Walk 100 feet in a straight line at a normal pace, counting the number of steps you take.
5. Calculate your stride length by dividing 100 by the number of steps you took. For example, if you took 40 steps, your stride length would be 2.5 feet.
Reprinted, by permission, from R.P. Pangrazi, 2007, *Pedometer power*, 2nd ed. (Champaign, IL: Human Kinetics), 64-65.
6. Set your pedometer stride length to match the number you calculated.
7. Wear your pedometer for two weeks during waking hours. Record your daily step counts and daily mileage and estimate the number of calories you expended.

Teacher Module 15.1 Pedometers   1
From *Physical Education Technology Playbook* by Darla Castelli and Leah Holland Fiorentino, 2008, Champaign, IL: Human Kinetics.

Teacher Module 15.1 Pedometers is available to download from the companion Web site.

Teacher Module 15.2
Heart Rate Monitors

Objective
To gather heart rate data using a Polar heart rate monitor and interpret the results using the Polar Heart Rate software that comes on the CD with the monitor.

National Standards for Beginning Physical Education Teachers
Standard 2 Growth and Development. Understand how individuals learn and develop, and provide opportunities that support physical, cognitive, social, and emotional development.
Standard 6 Planning and Instruction. Understand the importance of planning developmentally appropriate instructional units to foster the development of a physically educated person.
Standard 10 Collaboration. Understand the necessity of fostering collaborative relationships with colleagues, parents/guardians, and community agencies to support the development of a physically educated person.

Materials
*Computer workstations
*Polar heart rate monitors
*Computer interfaces

Discussion Questions
*Why is it important to consider or identify individual differences during physical activity?
*What new information about a student will a heart rate monitor provide to a teacher that would otherwise be inaccessible?

Directions
Unlike other modules, this module can be successfully completed using one of two options. The following directions apply to option 1.

Option 1
Polar x360 (infrared beam) heart rate monitors
Plot heart rate data from Polar software.
        *Collect heart rate data
        *Upload
        *Interpret
        *Summarize/recommendations/design

Directions for Option 1
1. Install the Polar Heart Rate software onto the computer and establish the Polar IR interface by connecting the infrared reader to the computer.
2. Properly place a Polar heart rate band around your chest so the center piece is over the tip of your sternum (xiphoid process). Make sure to moisten the monitor prior to putting it on.
Teacher Module 15.2 Heart Rate Monitors   1
From *Physical Education Technology Playbook* by Darla Castelli and Leah Holland Fiorentino, 2008, Champaign, IL: Human Kinetics.

Teacher Module 15.2 Heart Rate Monitors is available to download from the companion Web site.

Teacher Module 15.1 Pedometers

Teacher Module 15.2 Heart Rate Monitors

Because teachers who model appropriate behaviors to their students are more likely to achieve desired outcomes, the two teacher modules require that teachers use pedometers and heart rate monitors themselves. Teachers first wear pedometers for a two-week period, and then wear heart rate monitors for a single exercise session. In this way they become familiar with the setup and use of these technologies. The modules also require teachers to interpret the data they have collected.

Lesson Plan 15.1 Pedometers

The first lesson plan in this chapter encourages students to track personal physical activity engagement. By using pedometers to measure the number of steps they take, the distance they travel, or the calories they expend, students quantify their personal physical activity levels. Students are encouraged to set physical activity goals and attempt to meet those goals both during and beyond the school day.

Lesson Plan 15.1
Pedometers
Grades 4-6

Objective
To learn about the Mileage Club and have the opportunity to walk across America. A Mileage Club is a walking or running group that tracks how far the students travel. Some groups receive incentives for traveling certain distances, while others do not. See the Fitness Finders Web page (www.FitnessFinders.net) for more information on how you can establish your own club. Additionally, this lesson will help students learn what a pedometer is and how to use it.

National Standards for Physical Education
Standard 3: Participates regularly in physical activity.

Materials
*Pedometers
*Mileage Club log sheet (Create your own or use the version available from the Fitness Finders Web page.)

Accompanying File
LP15.1Student_Instructions

Set Induction
How long would it take you to walk from one end of this state to the other? How long would it take you to walk across the United States? How many miles is it? How many steps do you take in a mile? Over the course of this year, you will have the opportunity to record the number of steps you take in a mile and keep track of the number of miles you walk using your pedometer.

Activity
1. Explain the Mileage Club. It is a way to motivate students to be active outside of school by keeping track of how many steps they take throughout the day. When they reach the number of steps that indicates they have walked five miles, they record it on their log, have their parents sign it, and show you. They then receive a sticker for their log, which shows their progress toward walking across America.
2. Demonstrate to the students where the pedometer should be placed on their bodies to work properly. Remind them that a good place for the pedometer is on their waistband on the right side of their body, just under the hip bone. For some overweight children, you may need to slide the pedometer farther toward the side of their body, near their arms, but still securely placed on the waistband.
3. Teach the children how to reset the pedometer. Be sure to explain that they should reset the pedometer only when told to do so.
4. Some pedometers require the stride length to be calculated prior to use. See chapter 15 for more information about how to calculate the stride length.

Lesson Plan 15.1 Pedometers 1
From *Physical Education Technology Playbook* by Darla Castelli and Leah Holland Fiorentino, 2008, Champaign, IL: Human Kinetics.

Lesson Plan 15.1 Pedometers is available to download from the companion Web site.

Lesson Plan 15.2 Heart Rate Monitors

In this lesson, students will come to understand that different types of activities elicit different heart rates. Students will begin to integrate intensity into physical activity.

Lesson Plan 15.2
Heart Rate Monitors
Grades 6-12

Objective
To perform two different types of activities while wearing heart rate monitors, compare the different heart rates for each activity, and discuss and write an essay on which activity was more aerobic and why.

National Standards for Physical Education
Standard 3: Participates regularly in physical activity.

Materials
*Computer workstations
*Polar heart rate monitors
*Computer interfaces

Accompanying File
LP15.2Student_Instructions

Set Induction
What is a heart rate? When you exercise, what should your heart rate be? Are some activities more likely than others to increase your heart rate?

Activity
1. Make sure you have a heart rate monitor for each student. Assign each student a number that coincides with the number on his or her monitor. Each student will get a watch, a transmitter, and a strap.
2. Teach students the basics of how to put on the heart rate monitors before beginning the activities. If a monitor does not work, try the following troubleshooting tactics:
    a. Have the student exercise.
    b. Center the monitor by placing the watch in the middle of the transmitter.
    c. Adjust the strap and placement of the transmitter.
    d. Try using the watch with another transmitter or the transmitter with another watch.
    e. Consult the product's Web site for additional help and support.
3. Choose two activities, one more aerobic than the other, and have the class participate in both while wearing heart rate monitors. Examples of activities are jumping rope, football, volleyball, Frisbee, tennis, and weightlifting.
4. Have the students complete the different exercises and record their heart rates.
5. When everyone has had a chance to complete the heart rate exercises, discuss what this information means for training.

Lesson Plan 15.2 Heart Rate Monitors 1
From *Physical Education Technology Playbook* by Darla Castelli and Leah Holland Fiorentino, 2008, Champaign, IL: Human Kinetics.

Lesson Plan 15.2 Heart Rate Monitors is available to download from the companion Web site.

Keeping Up With Cutting-Edge Technologies and Long-Term Planning

s the students enter the weight room, they access their personalized workout plans on a PDA. The workouts have a "sticky note" (a virtual version of a self-stick note) reminder that the students should consider adding a new exercise to their routine to integrate the training principle of overload. To do this, students go to a permanent learning station in the weight room that contains an iPod. They put in the earbuds and select from a list of sample exercises that are available for display. These videos, created by older students in a media class, are examples for students in their first year at this school of how to resistance train. Over 50 audio and video files are accessible. As students exit the learning stations, you approach them to ask which exercise they are going to add to their program. You give them feedback about their choices and then observe their technique to facilitate proper technique. You teach the spotting technique, if necessary, and help them identify the appropriate starting weight and number of repetitions.

This chapter introduces some of the most recently integrated technologies: blogs, wikis, and podcasting. Each of these technologies is an interactive means of communicating via the Internet. Although teachers are not expected to create or develop these materials themselves, we introduce them as cutting-edge, integrated technologies that some teachers are already using in educational settings.

This chapter also helps teachers design long-term plans for keeping up with the latest technology. Teachers need to be vigilant about remaining current with technology, because what we embrace as cutting edge today will soon be commonplace. Continual technology upgrades and maintenance require creative, well-thought-out planning. This chapter encourages teachers to plan carefully to ensure that they have technology-savvy classrooms.

BLOGS

Blogs (Web logs) are one of the most recently integrated technologies to be applied in the educational setting. Blogs are like online diaries in which people share personal reflections on specific topics (e.g., employment, age, gender). In education, a blog can be a public place where a teacher can share reflections about teaching and learning. Information entered into blogs (opinions, beliefs, personal experiences) usually occurs chronologically and usually represents the thoughts of an individual over those of an organization. In addition to text, blogs can also contain pictures or podcasts (discussed later in this chapter).

As long as the Internet has been available to the public (since about 1994), there have been bloggers (those who use blogs), but it was not until the early 21st century that blogs became commonplace. Blogs are similar to Web pages in that they are housed on the Internet, but unlike Web pages they do not require a server. Instead, a variety of mechanisms can be used to create and maintain blogs. Free software such as w.bloggar (available for download from www.wbloggar.com) allows users to edit their own blogs using Microsoft Office from anywhere that they can access the Internet. This software is now compatible with both Internet Explorer and Mozilla Firefox browsers.

A few other Web sites permit people to set up their own blogs, but they are not without drawbacks. The Web site www.blogger.com, which is supported by Google, is very easy to use. Users just follow the icon steps, but they must first establish an account with Google, which may result in unwanted "pop-ups" and other notifications. Another blog site application, Type-Pad, is supported by the company Sixapart (www.sixapart.com). Again, there are drawbacks with the registration and sign-up.

Blogging Precautions

Some bloggers have been fired for illegally blogging during business hours as well as for posting opinions that differ from those of the organization. Despite the benefits of blogs, such as the sharing of wisdom obtained only through experience, the free-spirited nature common in the blogging world should be avoided in blogs that are integrated into educational settings. A blog that refers to a teacher's school, professional contact information, or employment responsibilities should be professionally formatted and maintained.

Professional education-related blogs share stories without identifying students or parents and are void of opinions that differ from school policy. The most effective teacher blogs are those that discuss the enactment of class projects and what helped or hindered implementation. As discriminating Web consumers, educators should first read other teacher blogs before creating their own. A blog maintained by an experienced teacher is a good place for a new teacher to get an insider's perspective on teaching and learning. Again, opinion-laden blogs should be created only on personal time; professional education-related blogs should contain primarily content knowledge and pedagogical suggestions.

WIKIS

A wiki is a piece of server software that allows users to freely create and edit Web page content using any Web browser. The development of a Web page typically requires Web editing or HTML editing software (see chapter 6 for a review of this content); however, a wiki can be modified using a Web browser, making collaboration highly interactive. A wiki is an unusual form of interaction in that it allows collaborators to contribute simultaneously to a body of work while communicating with all of the group members. This phenomenon is called open editing or collaborative authoring. The software allows all users to edit, add, or remove content from a Web page. The most popular version of a wiki is Wikipedia (www.wikipedia.org). Users can log on and add or remove content to the free online encyclopedia, thus making the content highly dynamic or organic, not static.

Wikis are used to collect collaborative thoughts from a group of people who are focused on completing a single project or a series of tasks requiring input from each member. Wikis are structured so that all group members have access to the latest version of the project. Contributions to the project are available immediately.

We recommend that beginners go to a free wiki builder called PBWiki (http://pbwiki.com/; see figure 16.1). From the home site, users type in the name of a project (using letters only) and their e-mail address. The PBWiki software goes to work creating a wiki. When the site is established, the details for continued access are sent to the submitted e-mail address. Users must log on to confirm that they want to use the wiki as the work space to complete their collaborative project.

PBWiki offers three templates to choose from: course syllabus, classroom, or group project. Users can also be brave and dive right in and create their own work space. The first step is to create a new page. At that point users are ready to create the work space (see figure 16.2 on page 106). We recommend that novices use one of the three templates.

Wikis are excellent for the quick exchange of ideas on a project that will likely require multiple drafts. Whether the project is designing the physical education Web page, developing long-term plans for lessons or curricula, or simply coordinating the use of the gymnasium space, wikis have an advantage over e-mail as the changes are immediately visible to the group members, and no one has to wait for members to respond. The best way to understand wikis is to create one and start working with a curious friend.

PODCASTING

Podcasting is a powerful tool that allows teachers to distribute audiovisual educational content to computers or portable media players (iPods) for learning on the go. After the initial investment in hardware, podcasting is a cost-effective way for schools and higher education institutions to share information. Many educators and institutions are already integrating podcasting into their curricula, because it permits them to use audio and video to enhance learning. The ability to combine text, audio, and images allows educators to address a variety of student learning styles.

Podcasting is not simply streaming video over the Internet. Because podcasts are downloadable to mobile devices, they have a broader range of dissemination. Podcasting uses a Really Simple

Figure 16.1 Peanut butter wiki.

Screenshot courtesy of PBwiki.com

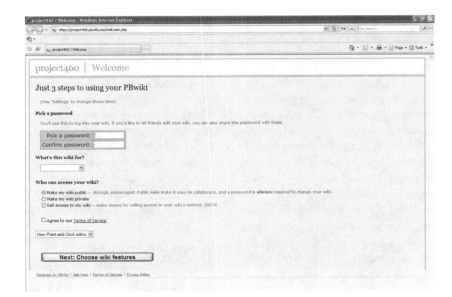

a

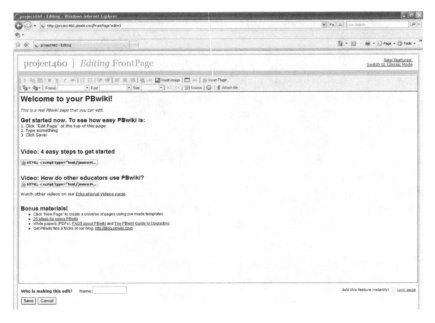

b

Figure 16.2 *a)* Using your wiki and *b)* Editing your wiki.

Screenshots courtesy of PBwiki.com

Syndication (RSS) format and XMTL technology to deliver content. These technologies allow anyone to publish content to the Internet to which interested parties can subscribe.

There are certain guidelines for podcasting that will ultimately determine its effectiveness. Less is more in the world of podcasting; video and audio segments should be brief, rarely exceeding eight minutes. Although podcasts have a tendency to be informal and even casual, their level of professionalism should be equal to or higher than that of the target audience. For example, a teacher in a podcast video should be professionally dressed and behave in a manner expected of a teacher. A teacher creating a podcast should never turn a webcam on himself in a hat and sunglasses sitting in his living room. Teacher-to-student podcasts require the same level of professionalism as lessons conducted in the classroom.

The audio on the podcast should be upbeat and positive, void of monotone speech. Because of the brevity of the segments, every clip should have meaning. As such, the teacher should select the content of a podcast carefully. To determine the appropriateness of content, the teacher should use strategies similar to those discussed in chapters 10 and 12 on digital capture and editing. Teacher podcasts should have a thematic approach to construction and format but also be flexible so as to include novel tasks or content as needed. A podcast should never be just a video of a class lecture. Each podcast should be less formal than a lecture, under eight minutes long, and provide teaching cues and reminders of what is expected of students.

The best way to get started with podcasting is through the use of a Macintosh computer suite of iPhotos, iMovie, and Garageband software. These programs, which come with the purchase of a Macintosh computer, are easy to use and well interfaced. Garageband helps the user add "voice-over" to video. It provides background music from redesigned loops or permits the user to develop music from scratch. Once audio has been added to the file, a user can publish the podcast directly from the Garageband software to iTunes. PC users can also create podcasts; however, software in this format is slightly more complex.

OVERCOMING BARRIERS RELATED TO TECHNOLOGY INTEGRATION

In a study of preservice physical education teacher attitudes toward technology education, many identified more barriers than facilitators to integration (Castelli & Fiorentino, 2004). Among the barriers cited were time, money, and the fear that the technologies would be permanently broken and not work if integrated. As suggested in the first two chapters of this book, if the integration of technology enhances teacher efficiency, fosters student learning, or presents content in a way in which it could not be delivered previously, then these barriers can and should be overcome.

In the beginning, teachers should select and master a single technology. Perhaps it is the use of a wiki to work on a curriculum. Teachers could also consider integrating pedometers, heart rate monitors, or the Fitnessgram/Activitygram program, which are easily aligned with learning objectives and the national physical education standards; any of these would be a logical first choice for integration. Whatever technology the

teacher selects, new doors will be opened because of the attempt to upgrade the physical education curriculum.

To remain current in technology and stay on top of the constant influx of updates to devices and tools, teachers must continually access information about new products and advances in applications. Professional growth and development are naturally extended through the integration of technology, because technology is not exclusively a device but also a process. Teacher learning does not stop with the earning of a degree; rather, it begins with certification.

LONG-TERM PLANNING AND INTEGRATION

Once a teacher is comfortable with a technology, a long-term plan for integration should begin. This plan involves four steps: *(1)* conduct a needs assessment, *(2)* develop a purchase plan, *(3)* align the technology with specific learning standards, and *(4)* plan for integration or implementation. This process assumes that the teacher has already attained the necessary skill to use the technology. In this way the teacher will not be an inhibitor to successful integration and maintenance.

Long-term plans begin with a needs assessment, which is an inventory of all teacher-accessible technology. This inventory should be electronic (e.g., a list of items on a spreadsheet) as well as physical. For example, an electronic inventory might indicate that four PDAs are available for use from the media center. When the teacher conducts a physical inventory, however, she discovers that two PDAs are missing power cords and only one has the Documents To Go software. A needs assessment may reveal that the teacher should sign out the camera, charge batteries, or purchase blank media. More likely, however, it will reveal that the teacher must make some additional purchases.

Development of a purchase plan is the next logical step following the needs assessment. The teacher will have to remain within the physical education budget or begin to identify external funding sources, such as the state AAHPERD organization or the parent–teacher organization. Although a teacher might like to purchase a heart rate monitor for each student in the class, it may be more realistic that only 10 students wear heart rate monitors in the first year of implementation. A teacher must realize that starting small is not a defeat, but an opportunity to begin attempts at attaining full technology integration goals.

During the next step in planning, the teacher should align the technology with the educational standard(s) he is looking to address. Helping students meet the standards is a valid reason for requesting additional funding for a technology that will foster student growth. During this step, the teacher should also consider pilot testing the selected technology. Ideally, he could conduct these pilots during the summer months; however, often the pilot will need to be done with a single class. The physical education teacher must justify the integration of technology in the curriculum as well as take part in professional development opportunities that will enhance productivity and learning.

As with all innovations, there are concerns about implementation. For example, creating a new Virtual Gym is time-consuming and requires advanced technology skills. It may be difficult to capture a high-quality video of specific game-play situations. Additionally, technologies such as those integrated in the Virtual Gym have been linked to decreases in physical activity among children. The challenge is for educators to think of better ways to use technology to improve physical activity levels and entice students to be more active.

The technologies described in this book are user-friendly and designed to increase student motivation. Educators need to promote a shift from sedentary, technology-related games to programs based on active, physical participation as the means to inspire continued play, both virtually and in real life. If technology's mission is to make tasks easier, then the natural application in physical education settings would be to use the latest available technology to encourage children to be more active and healthier on a regular basis. In summary, long-term planning is a four-step process of identifying, securing, aligning, and implementing various technologies.

CAVEATS OF THE NEXT BOOK EDITION

It is our intent to continue our personal and professional growth and publish subsequent editions of this text that reflect the integration of cutting-edge technology as physical education teachers upgrade both the devices themselves and the pedagogical processes related to their integration. For example, the next edition of this book will likely detail podcasting, wikis, and blogs, along with educational evidence demonstrating enhanced learning and efficiency as a result of these technologies (and perhaps new ones). The modifiable nature of the materials on the companion Web site allows teachers and teacher educators to create personalized modules for implementation. We welcome guest authors for new chapters in future editions. For example, if you are considered an expert on handheld devices, please feel free to contact us if you are interested in contributing to future editions of this text.

This book is intended to describe technologies that enhance learning, not simply evaluate products. Each of the modules has been used with preservice teachers or in K-12 physical education curricula. Some teachers expressed early concerns about the equipment and effort required to learn and apply the technology, but after actually using the technology (such as Virtual Gym), they agreed that accessing equipment was simple and that the technology was user-friendly. Additionally, teachers reported that Virtual Gym provided more opportunities for them to interact with students individually. Students offered teachers positive suggestions as well as personal perceptions about using Virtual Gym technology in physical education. Two themes emerged from students: (1) Virtual Gym is fun for all, regardless of skill level, and (2) they would like an opportunity to practice with Virtual Gym programs in all sport-related tasks. Students expressed the following positive comments about Virtual Gym:

> I would use it at home or in school.
> This is awesome. . . . Are we going to do this for all sports?
> Even though this one is not my favorite sport, I had fun with the video.
> Since I play on a travel team, it can make me get better.
> Some kids catch on fast and some need a little more time, but we all had a good time.

SUMMARY

Technology is ever-changing, and on the horizon are new and exciting cutting-edge devices that have the potential to be integrated into physical education curricula. When considering the integration of these technologies, however, teachers should consider the process as well as the justification for their use. Blogs, wikis, and podcasting have recently been applied to the educational context and will likely be shown to have a positive impact. Teachers need to include the evolution of technolo-gies in their long-term planning. An important step in planning is the alignment of standards to the technology and an inventory of what is presently available. External funds may be necessary for the teacher to fully integrate technology for the purpose of fostering learning and accomplishing something that has never been done before.

Technology Terms

Activitygram—As part of the Fitnessgram/Activitygram software package, Activitygram is a three-day assessment of student physical activity engagement. Physical activity is assessed in 30 blocks, based on the type, intensity, and length of activity. The software can generate a physical activity report. (The program is available from Human Kinetics.)

attachment—A file attached to an e-mail message. Many e-mail systems support sending only text files as e-mail. If the attachment is a binary file or formatted text file (such as a Microsoft Word document), it must be encoded before it is sent and decoded once it is received. Other systems allow images and multiple types of files to be attached to an e-mail message as well.

backslash—The backslash character is \; a simple slash, or forward slash, is /. In DOS and Windows systems, the backslash represents the root directory and is also used to separate directory names and file names in a path name, or a sequence of symbols and names that identifies a file. Every file has a name, called a file name, so the simplest type of path name is just a file name. In DOS systems, for example, the root directory is named \, and each subdirectory is separated by an additional backslash. In UNIX, the root directory is named /, and each subdirectory is followed by a slash. In Macintosh environments, directories are separated by a colon.

binary—Pertaining to a number system that has just two digits. For most purposes, we use the decimal number system, which has 10 digits, 0 through 9. All other numbers are then formed by combining these 10 digits. Computers are based on the binary numbering system, which consists of just two numbers, 0 and 1. All operations that are possible in the decimal system (addition, subtraction, multiplication, division) are equally possible in the binary system.

blog—An online journal which displays chronologically occurring events as they are reported by the individual maintaining the blog.

bookmark—The act of saving a URL for future reference.

boot—To load the first piece of software that starts a computer. Because the operating system is essential for running all other programs, it is usually the first piece of software loaded during the boot process, which involves loading the operating system and other basic software. A cold boot is turning the computer on from an off position. A warm boot is resetting a computer that is already on.

browser—Short for *Web browser,* a software application used to locate and display Web pages. The two most popular browsers are Netscape Navigator and Microsoft Internet Explorer. Both are graphical browsers, which means that they can display graphics as well as text. In addition, most modern browsers can present multimedia information, including sound and video, although they require plug-ins for some formats.

click—To tap on a mouse button, pressing it down and then immediately releasing it. Note that clicking a mouse button is different from pressing (or dragging) a mouse button, which implies holding the button down without releasing it, in order to transfer an object with the cursor to a desired location. The phrase *to click on* means to select a screen object by moving the mouse pointer to the object's position and clicking a mouse button. Some operations require a double click, which involves clicking a mouse button twice in rapid succession; this opens an application.

clipboard—A special file or memory area (buffer) where data are stored temporarily before being copied to another location. Many word processors, for example, use a clipboard for cutting and pasting. When a block of text is copied, the word processor copies the block to the clipboard; when the block is pasted, the word processor copies it from the clipboard to its final destination. In Microsoft Windows and the Apple Macintosh operating system, the Clipboard (with a capital *C*) can be used to copy data from one application to another.

CPU—Abbreviation of *central processing unit,* and pronounced as separate letters. The CPU is the brains of the computer. Sometimes referred to simply as the processor or central processor, the CPU is where most calculations take place. In terms of computing power, the CPU is the most important element of a computer system. On large machines, CPUs require one or more printed circuit boards. On personal computers and small workstations, the CPU is housed in a single chip called a microprocessor.

cursor—A special symbol, usually a solid rectangle or a blinking underline character, that signifies where the next character will be displayed on the screen. To type in different areas of the screen, one must move the cursor. This is done with the arrow keys or with a mouse if the program supports it. In graphics-based programs, the cursor may appear as a small arrow, called a pointer. (The terms *cursor* and *pointer* are often used interchangeably.) In text processing, a cursor sometimes appears as an I-beam pointer, a special type of pointer that always appears between two characters. Note also that programs that support a mouse may use two cursors: a text cursor, which indicates where characters from the keyboard will be entered, and a mouse cursor for selecting items with the mouse.

data—Distinct pieces of information that are organized by categories. These can appear as text, numeric, or alpha-numeric code.

data entry—The process of entering data into a computerized database or spreadsheet. Data entry can be performed by an individual typing at a keyboard or by a machine entering data electronically. (Taken from the online encyclopedia webopedia [www.webopedia. com/TERM/D/data_entry.html])

database—A collection of information organized in such a way that a computer program can quickly select desired pieces of data. A database is like an electronic filing system. Traditional databases are organized by fields, records, and files. A field is a single piece of information; a record is one complete set of fields; and a file is a collection of records. An alternative concept in database design is known as hypertext. In a hypertext database, any object, whether it is a piece of text, a picture, or a film, can be linked to any other object. A database management system (DBMS) is needed to access information from a database. This is a collection of programs that enables a person to enter, organize, and select data in a database.

default—A value or setting that a device or program automatically selects when a substitute is not specified. For example, word processors have default margins and default page lengths that one can override or reset. The default drive is the disk drive the computer accesses unless a different disk drive is specified. Likewise, the default directory is the directory the operating system searches unless a different directory is specified.

desktop—In graphical user interfaces, a desktop is the metaphor used to portray file systems. A desktop consists of pictures, called icons, that show cabinets, files, folders, and various types of documents or images. The icons on the electronic desktop can be arranged just as real objects on a real desktop can—by moving them around, putting one on top of another, reshuffling them, and throwing them away.

dialogue box—A box that appears on a display screen to present information or request input. Typically, dialogue boxes are temporary; they disappear once the requested information has been entered. This window, when open, will not close until the user has performed some sort of action. Examples include the *Open File* dialogue box, the *Save File* dialogue box, and the *Print* dialogue box.

download—To copy data (usually an entire file) from a main source to a peripheral device. The term is often used to describe the process of copying a file from an online service or bulletin board service (BBS) to one's own computer. Downloading can also refer to copying a file from a network file server to a computer on the network. The opposite of *download* is *upload,* which means to copy a file from one's own computer to another computer.

e-mail—Short for *electronic mail,* the transmission of messages over communications networks. The messages can be notes entered from the keyboard or electronic files stored on disk. Some e-mail systems are confined to a single computer system or network, but others have gateways to other computer systems, enabling users to send electronic mail anywhere in the world. Message are sent by specifying the recipient's address. The same message can also be sent to several users at once. This is called broadcasting. Sent messages are stored in electronic mailboxes until the recipient fetches them. After reading an e-mail, a person can store it in a text file, forward it to other users, or delete it.

Fitnessgram—As part of the Fitnessgram/Activitygram software package, Fitnessgram converts fitness test scores into an evaluation of aerobic capacity, muscle fitness, and body composition. The software can generate a physical fitness report based on the healthy fitness zone criteria. (The program is available from Human Kinetics.)

folder—In graphical user interfaces such as Windows and the Macintosh environment, a folder is an object that can contain multiple documents. Folders are used to organize information. In the DOS and UNIX worlds, folders are called directories.

format control—The on-screen arrangement of how information is entered into the computer (e.g., text entered on a keyboard, text editing, or graphic interaction).

FTP—Abbreviation of *file transfer protocol,* the protocol used to upload files from a workstation to an FTP server or download files from an FTP server to a workstation. It is the way files get transferred from one device to another in order to be available on the Internet. When "ftp" appears in a URL, it means that the user is connecting to a file server and not a Web server and that some form of file transfer is going to take place. Most FTP servers require the user to log on to the server to transfer files. FTP is a two-way system: Files are transferred back and forth between the server and the workstation.

GIF—A layered picture. Often appears as animation.

gigabyte—A measurement of disk storage space. One gigabyte (GB) is equal to approximately 1 billion bytes.

hard disk—A magnetic disk on which computer data are stored. The term *hard* is used to distinguish it from a soft, or floppy, disk. Hard disks hold more data and are faster than floppy disks. A hard disk, for example, can store anywhere from 10 megabytes to several gigabytes of information, whereas most floppies have a maximum storage capacity of 1.4 megabytes.

home page—Generally the main page of a Web server.

HTML—Short for *hypertext markup language,* the authoring language used to create documents on the World Wide Web. HTML defines the structure and layout of a Web document by using a variety of tags (commands inserted in a document that specify how the document, or a portion of the document, should be formatted) and attributes, or characteristics.

HTTP—Short for *hypertext transfer protocol,* the underlying protocol used by the World Wide Web. HTTP defines how messages are formatted and transmitted and what actions Web servers and browsers should take in response to various commands. This protocol is used to transfer files from a Web server onto a browser to view a Web page that is on the Internet. Unlike FTP, where entire files are transferred from one device to another and copied into memory, HTTP transfers only the contents of a Web page into a browser for viewing. HTTP is a one-way system: Files are transported only from the server onto the workstation's browser. When "http" appears in a URL, it means that the user is connecting to a Web server and not a file server. The files are transferred but not downloaded or copied into the memory of the receiving device.

hypertext—A system in which objects (text, pictures, music, programs) can be creatively linked to each other. When an object is selected, all the other objects that are linked to it are visible. The icons selected to view associated objects are called hypertext links or buttons.

icon—A small picture that represents an object or program. Icons are very useful in applications that use Windows, because with the click of a mouse button, users can shrink an entire window into a small icon. (This is sometimes called minimizing.) To redisplay the window, the user merely moves the pointer to the icon and clicks (or double-clicks) a mouse button. (This is sometimes called restoring or maximizing.) Icons are a principal feature of graphical user interfaces.

interface—How interdependent systems communicate with one another.

Internet—A worldwide network that connects many smaller networks with a common set of procedures (protocols) for sending and receiving information.

ISP—Short for *Internet service provider,* a company that provides access to the Internet. The service provider offers a software package, user name, password, and access phone number. Equipped with a modem, a user can then log on to the Internet and browse the World Wide Web and USENET (a worldwide bulletin board system that can be accessed through the Internet or through many online services), and send and receive e-mail. In addition to serving individuals, ISPs also serve large companies, providing a direct connection from the company's networks to the Internet.

JavaScript—Originally called OAK, it is a high-level programming language developed by Sun Microsystems. It has become popular for its ability to create interactive graphics and animation on Web pages.

JPEG (Joint Photographic Experts Group)—A file format for storing and sending graphic images on a network.

link—In some operating systems (UNIX, for example), a link is a pointer to a file. Links make it possible to reference a file by several different names and to access a file without specifying a full path. In hypertext systems, such as the World Wide Web, a link is a reference to another document. Such links are sometimes called hot links because they take users to the other document when they click on them.

maximize—In graphical user interfaces, to enlarge a window to its maximum size. In Windows and Macintosh environments, the buttons for minimizing and maximizing windows are located in the top right corner of the window.

minimize—In graphical user interfaces, to convert a window into an icon.

MPEG (Motion Picture Experts Group)—A file format for storing and sending video sequences on a network.

network—A group of two or more computer systems linked together. Computers and devices that allocate resources for a network are called servers. There are many types of computer networks, including local area networks (LANs), wide area networks (WANs), campus area networks (CANs), metropolitan area networks (MANs), and home area networks (HANs).

search engines—Internet software (e.g., Google, Excite) that helps people locate Internet sites and information related to a given topic.

server—A computer or device on a network that manages network resources. For example, a file server is a computer and storage device dedicated to storing files. Any user on the network can store files on the server. A print server is a computer that manages one or more printers, and a network server is a computer that manages network traffic. A database server is a computer system that processes database queries.

software—Computer instructions or data. Anything that can be stored electronically is software. The storage devices and display devices are hardware. The distinction between software and hardware is sometimes confusing because they are so integrally linked. Clearly, when a person purchases a program, she is buying software. But to buy the software, she must buy the disk (hardware) on which the software is recorded. Systems software includes the operating system and all the utilities that enable the computer to function. Applications software includes programs that do real work for users; for example, word processors, spreadsheets, and database management systems.

spreadsheet—Software designed to store data (usually, but not always, numeric) by row-column positions known as *cells*; can also do calculations on the data.

systems tray—Located in the Windows taskbar (usually at the bottom of the screen, next to the clock), it contains miniature icons for easy access to system functions such as fax, printer, modem, volume, and more. A person double-clicks or right-clicks on an icon to view and access the details and controls.

target—Synonymous with *destination,* a target is a file, device, or any type of location to which data are moved or copied. Many computer commands involve copying data from one place to another (from one source to a target).

task bar—An operating system concept that refers to the combination of a program being executed and bookkeeping information used by the operating system. Whenever a program is executed, the operating system creates a new task for it. Many operating systems, including UNIX, OS/2, and Windows, are capable of running many tasks at the same time and are called multitasking operating systems. The task bar (often at the bottom of the screen) includes the start menu, currently opened windows, and the systems tray.

telnet—A terminal emulation program for TCP/IP networks such as the Internet. The telnet program runs on a computer and connects the PC to a server on the network. A person can then enter commands through the telnet program, and they will be executed as if he had entered them directly on the server console. This enables the person to control the server and communicate with other servers on the network. To start a telnet session, a person must log in to a server by entering a valid user name and password. Telnet is a common way to control Web servers remotely.

terabyte—A measurement of disk storage space. One terabyte (TB) equals approximately 1 trillion bytes of storage space.

title bar—A bar on top of a window. The title bar contains the name of the file or application. In many graphical user interfaces, including the Macintosh and Microsoft Windows interfaces, the user moves (drags) a window by grabbing the title bar. The title bar contains the name of the window; the system menu; and the minimize, maximize, and close options.

toolbar—A series of selectable buttons in a computer graphics interface that gives the user an easy way to select desktop, application, or Web browser functions. A toolbar is typically displayed as either a horizontal row or a vertical column, generally sharing a theme, around the edges of the graphical user interface where it is visible while the application is in use. Most applications use toolbars because they give the user another option aside from pull-down menus.

Transmission Control Protocol/Internet Protocol (TCP/IP)—A standard, agreed-upon way of coding and sending data across the Internet.

URL—Abbreviation of *uniform resource locator,* the global address of a document or other resource on the World Wide Web. The first part of the address indicates what protocol to use, and the second part specifies the IP address or the domain name where the resource is located. The URL www.adelphi.edu points to a file at the domain adelphi.edu. It specifies a Web page that should be fetched using the HTTP.

user name—A name used to gain access to a computer system. User names, and often passwords, are required in multiuser systems. In most such systems, users can choose their own user names and passwords.

Web browsers—Software that allows users to navigate and search the World Wide Web, such as Internet Explorer, Netscape, Mozilla Firefox, and Opera.

Web browsing—"Wandering," "surfing," or "navigating" the World Wide Web.

Web page—A specific file location on the World Wide Web identified with a uniform resource locator (URL).

Web site—A series of related Web pages that are connected through a home page and are physically located on a server connected to the Internet.

Wikipedia—A free encyclopedia built collaboratively using wiki software.

wikis—An editable Web page that reflects the collaborative efforts of a group. Each group member has access to and is capable of editing the contents of the Web page. Can be used to complete team projects or simply as a means of communication.

World Wide Web (WWW)—A system of Internet servers that supports specially formatted documents. The documents are formatted in a script called HTML that supports links to other documents, as well as graphics, audio, and video files. This means that a person can jump from one document to another simply by clicking on a hot spot, or an area that activates a function. Users access Web documents (called Web pages) on the WWW using browsers, such as Internet Explorer and Netscape. The Web pages are linked to each other via hyperlinks. Not all Internet servers are part of this system. The World Wide Web is not synonymous with the Internet. The World Wide Web, or simply the Web, is a way of accessing information over the medium of the Internet. It is an information-sharing model that is built on top of the Internet.

References and Resources

Abdal-Haqq, I. (1995). Infusing technology into preservice teacher education. ERIC Digest. (ERIC Document Reproduction Service No. ED 389 699.)

Albion, P.R. (2001). Some factors in the development of self-efficacy beliefs for computer use among teacher education students. *Journal of Technology and Teacher Education, 9* (3), 321-347.

American College of Sports Medicine. (2006). *ACSM's guidelines for exercise testing and prescription* (7th ed.). New York: Lippincott Williams & Wilkins.

Armstrong, T. (2000). *Multiple intelligences in the classroom* (2nd ed.). Alexandria, VA: Association for Supervision and Curriculum Development.

Bandura, A. (1997). *Self-efficacy: The exercise of control.* New York: Freeman.

Baron, L.C. & Goldman, E.S. (1994). Integrating technology with teacher preparation. In B. Means (Ed.), *Technology and education reform: The reality behind the promise.* Hoboken, NJ: Jossey-Bass, 81-110.

Battle-Bailey, L. (2004). Interactive homework for increasing parent involvement and student reading achievement. *Childhood Education, 81* (1), 36.

Beck, R.J. (2000). *A narrative inquiry of computer supported collaborative learning in a preservice teacher peer group.* Washington, DC: U.S. Department of Education.

Blakemore, C. (2004). Brain research strategies for physical educators. *Journal of Physical Education, Recreation, and Dance, 75* (1), 31-36.

Brahler, C.J., Quitadamo, I.J. & Johnson, E.C. (2002). Student critical thinking is enhanced by developing exercise prescriptions using online learning modules. *Advances in Physiology Education, 26* (3), 210-221.

Bronfenbrenner, U. (1977). Toward an experimental ecology of human development. *American Psychologist, 32,* 513-531.

Bryan, J., Osendarp, S., Hughes, D., Calvaresi, E., Baghurst, K. & van Klinken, J.W. (2004). Nutrients for cognitive development in school-aged children. *Nutrition Reviews, 62* (8), 295-306.

Castelli, D.M. (Ed.). (2005). Technology integration, virtually possible. *Teaching Elementary Physical Education, 16* (5), 6-7.

Castelli, D.M. & Fiorentino, L. (2004). The effects of different instruction on preservice teacher perceived ability and comfort with technology in physical education. *Research Quarterly for Exercise and Sport, 75* (1), 63.

Castelli, D.M., Hillman, C.H., Buck, S.E. & Erwin, H.E. (2007). Physical fitness and academic achievement in 3rd and 5th grade students. *Journal of Sport & Exercise Psychology, 29* (2), 239-252.

Castelli, D.M. & Rink, J. (2003). Chapter 3: A comparison of high- and low-performing secondary physical education programs. *Journal of Teaching in Physical Education, 22* (5), 512-521.

Christakis, D.A., Ebel, B.E., Rivara, F.P. & Zimmerman, F.J. (2004). Television, video, and computer game usage in children under 11 years of age. *The Journal of Pediatrics, 145,* 652-656.

Coe, D.P., Pivarink, J.M., Womack, C.J., Reeves, M.J. & Malina, R.M. (2006). Effects of physical education and activity levels on academic achievement in children. *Medicine & Science in Sports & Exercise, 38* (8), 1515-1559.

Corbin, C.B., Pangrazi, R.P. & Le Masurier, G.C. (2004). Physical activity for children: Current patterns and guidelines. *President's Council on Physical Fitness and Sports Research Digest, 5* (2), 1-8.

Crawford, C.M. (2000). Collected papers on graduate and inservice teacher education and technology. *Proceedings of SITE (Society for Information Technology and Teacher Education International Conference) 2000.* (ERIC Document Reproduction Service No. ED 444 498.)

Curtis, M., Kopera, J., Norris, C. & Solloway, E. (2004). *Palm OS handhelds in the elementary classroom: Curriculum and strategies*. Washington, DC: International Society for Technology in Education [ISTE].

Curtis, M., Williams, B., Norris, C., O'Leary, D. & Soloway, E. (2003). *Palm handheld computers: A complete resource for classroom teachers*. Washington, DC: ISTE Publications.

Dale, D. & Corbin, C. (2000). Physical activity of high school graduates following exposure to conceptual or traditional physical education. *Research Quarterly for Exercise and Sport, 71* (1), 61-68.

Datar, A., Sturm, R. & Magnabosco, J. L. (2004). Childhood overweight and academic performance: National study of kindergartners and first-graders. *Obesity Research, 12* (1), 58-68.

Dexter, S.L., Anderson, R.E. & Becker, H.J. (1999). Teachers' views of computers as catalysts for changes in their teaching practice. *Journal of Research on Computing in Education, 31* (3), 221-239.

Dodge, B. (2006a). Some thoughts about Web Quests. Retrieved from http://edweb.sdsu.edu/courses/edtec596/about_webquests.html.

Dodge, B. (2006b). What's a Web Quest? Retrieved from http://webquest.sdsu.edu/overview.htm.

Ertmer, P.A., Gopalakrishnan, S. & Ross, E.M. (2001). Technology-using teachers: Comparing perceptions of exemplary technology use to best practice. *Journal of Research on Technology in Education, 33* (5), 1-18.

Fiorentino, L.H. & Castelli, D.M. (2005a). Creating a virtual gymnasium: Providing an opportunity for perfect practice. *Journal of Physical Education, Recreation, and Dance, 76* (4), 16-18.

Fiorentino, L. & Castelli, D.M. (2005b). The virtual gymnasium: An innovative approach to the development of perfect practice situations. *Contemporary Issues in Technology and Teacher Education, 5* (1), 1-5.

Fontaine, K.R., Redden, D.T., Wang, C., Westfall, A.O. & Allison, D.B. (2003). Years of life lost due to obesity. *Journal of the American Medical Association, 289* (2), 187-193.

Freidus, H. & Grose, C. (1998). *Implementing curriculum change: Lessons from the field*. Paper presented at the Annual Meeting of the American Educational Research Association, San Diego, CA. (ERIC Document Reproduction Service No. ED 422 606.)

Gardner, H. (1997). *Frames of mind: The theory of multiple intelligences*. New York: Basic Books.

Gillingham, M.G. & Topper, A. (1999). Technology in teacher preparation: Preparing teachers for the future. *Journal of Technology and Teacher Education, 7* (4), 303-321.

Gordon-Larsen, P., Nelson, M.C. & Popkin, B.M. (2004). Longitudinal physical activity and sedentary behavior trends: Adolescence to adulthood. *American Journal of Preventive Medicine, 27* (4), 277-283.

Hancock, D.R., Bray, M. & Nason, S.A. (2002). Influencing university students' achievement and motivation in a technology course. *Journal of Educational Research, 95,* 365-372.

Hargrave, C.P. & Hsu, Y.S. (2000). Survey of instructional technology courses for preservice teachers. *Journal of Technology and Teacher Education, 8* (4), 303-314.

Hedley, A.A., Ogden, C.L., Johnson, C.L., Carroll, M.D., Curtin, L.R. & Flegal, K.M. (2004). Prevalence of overweight and obesity among U.S. children, adolescents, and adults, 1999-2002. *JAMA.* 2004;291: 2847-2850.

Holt/Hale, S.A. (1999). *Assessing motor skills in elementary physical education*. Reston, VA: National Association for Sport and Physical Education.

Hopper, C.A., Munoz, K.O., Gruber, M.B. & Nguyen, K.P. (2005). The effects of a family program on the physical activity and nutrition behaviors of third-grade children. *Research Quarterly for Exercise and Sport, 76,* 130-139.

House Education and Workforce Committee. (2004). Child Nutrition and WIC Reauthorization Act. Retrieved from http://edworkforce.house.gov/issues/108th/education/childnutrition/billsummaryfinal.htm.

International Society for Technology in Education & U.S. Department of Education. (2003). *National educational technology: Standards for teachers*. Washington, DC: Authors.

Jones, D.L. & Garrahy, D. (2001). Preservice teachers' perceptions regarding the use of computers in supervising an elementary physical education field experience. *Research Quarterly for Exercise and Sport, 72* (1), A-68.

Kaiser Family Foundation. (2005). Generation M: Media in the lives of 8- to 18-year-olds. Retrieved from www.kff.org.

Kaiser Family Foundation. (2004). Role of media in childhood obesity. Retrieved from www.kff.org/entmedia/upload/The-Role-Of-Media-in-Childhood-Obesity.pdf.

Kirkpatrick, B. (1997). *Lessons from the heart: Individualizing physical dducation with heart rate monitors*. Champaign, IL: Human Kinetics.

Kulik, J. (1994). Meta-analytic studies of findings on computer-based instruction. In E.L. Baker and

H.F. O'Neil, Jr. (Eds.), *Technology assessment in education and training.* Hillsdale, NJ: Lawrence Erlbaum, 9-33.

Kulinna, P.H. & Silverman, S. (2000). Teachers' attitudes toward teaching physical activity and fitness. *Research Quarterly for Exercise and Sport, 71* (1), 80-84.

Lagone, C., Wissick, C., Langone, J. & Ross, G. (1998). A study of graduates of a technology teacher preparation program. *Journal of Technology and Teacher Education, 6* (4), 283-302.

Liu, M., Reed, M. & Phillips, P.D. (1990). *Teacher education students and computers: Gender, major, use, occurrence, and anxiety.* Paper presented at the Annual Meeting of the American Educational Research Association. Boston, MA. (ERIC Document Reproduction Service No. ED 324 338.)

Lonergan, J. (2001). Preparing urban teachers to use technology for instruction. ERIC Clearinghouse on Urban Education. New York, NY. Pg. 1-7. (ERIC Document Reproduction Service No. ED 460 190.)

Lynn, S.K., Castelli, D.M., Werner, P. & Cane, S.L. (2007). *Seminar in physical education: From student teaching to teaching students.* Champaign, IL: Human Kinetics, 189-190.

March, T. (2006a). Web Quests for learning: Why Web Quests? An introduction. Retrieved from www.ozline.com/webquests/intro.html.

March, T. (2006b). Best Web Quests. Retrieved from www.ozline.com.

Marcinkiewicz, H.R. (1993). Computers and teachers: Factors influencing computer use in the classroom. *Journal of Research on Computing in Education, 26* (2), 220-236.

Marshall, S.J., Biddle, S.J.H., Gorely, T., Cameron, N. & Murdey, I. (2004). Relationships between media use, body fatness and physical activity in children and youth: A meta-analysis. *International Journal of Obesity, 28,* 1238-1246.

Martin, J. J., Kulinna, P. & Cothran, D. (2002). Motivating students through assessment. *Journal of Physical Education, Recreation, and Dance, 73,* 18-19, 30.

Massare, D.W. & Cowan, N. (2006). Information processing: Microscopes of the mind. *Annual Reviews of Psychology, 44,* 383-425.

Mohnsen, B. (2008). *Using technology in physical education* (6th ed.). Cerritos, CA: Bonnie's Fitware Inc.

Morley, L. (1999). Expanding preservice teachers' tools for effective teaching. National Conference on Technology in Physical Education and Sport, 2-6. (ERIC Document Reproduction Service No. ED 432 548.)

Moursund, D. & Bielefeldt, T. (1999). Will new teachers be prepared to teach in a digital age? A national survey on information technology in teacher education. Eugene, OR: International Society for Technology in Education [ISTE]. (ERIC Document Reproduction Service No. ED 428 072.)

National Association for Sport and Physical Education. (2004). *Physical activity for children. A statement of guidelines for children ages 5-12* (2nd ed.). Reston, VA: Author.

National Association for Sport and Physical Education. (2001). Standards for initial programs in physical education teacher education. Retrieved from www.aahperd.org/naspe/pdf.files/standards_initial.pdf, 1-29.

National Center for Education Statistics [NCES]. (2000). *Teachers' tools for the 21st century: A report on teachers' use of technology.* Washington, DC: Author. Retrieved from http://nces.ed.gov/surveys/frss/publications/2000102/index.asp.

National Center for Education Statistics [NCES]. (1999). National assessment of educational progress 1999 trends in academic progress: Three decades of student performance. *Education Statistics Quarterly, 2* (4) Topic: Elementary and Secondary Education. Retrieved from http://nces.ed.gov/programs/quarterly/Vol_2/2_4/e_section2.asp.

Pangrazi, R., Beighle, A. & Sidman, C. (2007). *Pedometer power* (2nd ed.). Champaign, IL: Human Kinetics.

Rink, J. (2005). *Teaching physical education for learning.* (5th ed.). Boston: McGraw-Hill.

Rink, J. (2004). It's okay to be a beginner. *Journal of Physical Education, Recreation, and Dance, 75* (6), 31-34.

Rink, J. & Mitchell, M. (2003). State level assessment in physical education: The South Carolina experience. *Journal of Teaching in Physical Education, 22,* 471-493.

Roblyer, M.D. (2003). *Integrating educational technology into teaching* (3rd ed.). Upper Saddle River, NJ: Pearson Education.

Roblyer, M.D. (1993). Why use technology in teaching? Making a case beyond research results. *Florida Technology in Education Quarterly, 5* (4), 7-13.

Sallis, J. F. & Owen, N. (1997). Ecological models. In K. Glanz, F. M. Lewis & B. K. Rimer (Eds.) *Health behavior and health education: Theory, research, and practice* (2nd ed.), 403-424. San Francisco: Jossey-Bass.

Sallis, J.F., Prochaska, J.J. & Taylor, W.C. (2000). A review of correlates of physical activity of children and adolescents. *Medicine & Science in Sports &*

Exercise, 32 (5), 963-975.

Sandholtz, J.H. (2001). Learning to teach with technology: A comparison of teacher development programs. *Journal of Technology and Teacher Education, 9* (3), 349-374.

Senne, T.A. & Rikard, G.L. (2002). Experiencing the portfolio process during the internship: A comparative analysis of two PETE portfolio models. *Journal of Teaching in Physical Education, 21,* 309-336.

Siedentop, D., Hastie, P.A. & van der Mars, H. (2005). *Complete guide to sport education.* Champaign, IL: Human Kinetics.

Soloway, E. & Norris, C. (2006). Research shows handheld computers in classrooms enhance student achievement. Ann Arbor, MI: GoKnow Learning. Retrieved from www.goknow.com/sbr/GoKnow%20SBR%20Announcement.pdf.

Strong, W.B., Malina, R.M., Blimkie, C.J., Daniels, S.R., Dishman, R.K., Gutin, B., et al. (2005). Evidence based physical activity for school-age youth. *Journal of Pediatrics, 146,* 732-737.

Stuhlmann, J.M. (1998). A model for infusing technology into teaching training programs. *Journal of Technology and Teacher Education, 6* (3), 125-139.

Taylor, H., & Wiebe. (1994, Spring). National standards for computer/technology teacher preparation: A catalyst for change in American education. *Journal of Computing in Teacher Education, 10* (3), 21-23.

Trost, S.G., Pate, R.R., Sallis, J.F., Freedson, P.S., Taylor, W.C., Dowda, M., et al. (2002). Age and gender differences in objectively measured physical activity in youth. *Medicine & Science in Sports & Exercise, 34* (2), 350-355.

U.S. Department of Education. (2000). *Teachers' tools for the 21st century: A report on teachers' use of technology.* Washington, DC: National Center for Education Statistic. Retrieved from http://nces. ed.gov/surveys/frss/publications/2000102/index. asp.

U.S. Department of Health and Human Services. (2000). Healthy people 2010: Understanding and improving health. Washington, DC: U.S. Government Printing Office. Retrieved from www.healthypeople.gov/Document/tableofcontents.htm#under.

Williams, K. (2004). What's motor development got to do with physical education? *Journal of Physical Education, Recreation, and Dance, 75* (6), 35-39.

Worrell, V., Evans-Fletcher, C. & Kovar, S. (2002). Assessing the cognitive and affective progress of children. *Journal of Physical Education, Recreation, & Dance, 73* (7), 29-34.

ADDITIONAL WEB RESOURCES

▶ Ourmedia.org—a site that will host your multimedia for free provided that you are willing for your content to be publicly available for use by others.

▶ iTunes—a downloadable, cross-program platform that provides easy access to podcasts and a lot more, with easy syncing to iPods. Downloaded from www.apple.com/itunes/.

▶ The Podcast RSS Buddy—a cross-platform shareware tool for producing RSS feeds, including iTunes compatible feeds. www.tolley.info/rssbuddy/tutorialV3.html.

About the Authors

Darla M. Castelli, PhD, is an assistant professor at the University of Illinois at Urbana-Champaign. She taught physical education in public schools for 10 years before becoming a teacher educator. In 1995 she was named Teacher of the Year by the Maine Association for Health, Physical Education, Recreation and Dance (AHPERD) and was named Illinois AHPERD Past President's Scholar in 2007. Dr. Castelli has received numerous awards, including the *Contemporary Issues in Technology and Teacher Education Journal* Gallery of Exemplary Use of Technology Award in 2004 for her design of the technology course at the University of Illinois. In her leisure time, she enjoys physical activity with her children, outdoor pursuits, and photography.

Leah Holland Fiorentino, EdD, is an assistant dean in the college of education at Armstrong Atlantic State University in Savannah, Georgia. She has been an invited speaker at national and international conferences on the topic of technology integration in teacher preparation programs and has designed and implemented technology integration plans in teacher education departments in several universities. Dr. Fiorentino has also created and taught introductory and advanced technology application courses since 1997 and has presented technology workshops at state, regional, and national conferences each year since 1999. She also won the *Contemporary Issues in Technology and Teacher Education Journal* Gallery of Exemplary Uses of Technology Award in 2004.

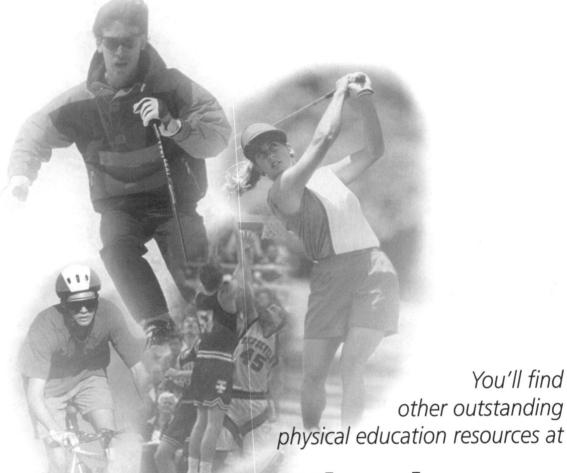

*You'll find
other outstanding
physical education resources at*

www.HumanKinetics.com

In the U.S. call

1-800-747-4457

Australia..08 8372 0999
Canada 1-800-465-7301
Europe...+44 (0) 113 255 5665
New Zealand......................................0064 9 448 1207

HUMAN KINETICS
The Information Leader in Physical Activity
P.O. Box 5076 • Champaign, IL 61825-5076 USA

How to access the companion Web site

We are pleased to provide access to a companion Web site that supplements your textbook, *Physical Education Technology Playbook*. This companion Web site offers teacher modules, lesson plans, and student instructions available to download and modify for use in your classroom.

Accessing the companion Web site is easy! Simply follow these steps:

1. Using your Web browser, go to the **Physical Education Technology Playbook** product Web site at **www.HumanKinetics.com/ PhysicalEducationTechnologyPlaybook**.

2. Click on the **View Ancillary Resources** button on the left side of the home page.

3. Click on the please register now link. You will create your personal profile and password at this time.

4. Write your e-mail and password down for future reference. Keep it in a safe place.

5. Once you are registered, enter the key code exactly as it is printed at the right, including all hyphens. Click **Submit**

6. Once the key code has been submitted, you will see a welcome screen. Click the **Continue** button to open your ancillary resources.

7. After you enter the key code the first time, you will not need to use it again to access the ancillary resources. In the future, simply log in using your e-mail and the password you created.

For technical support, send an e-mail to:
support@hkusa.com . . . . U.S. and international customers
info@hkcanada.com . . . . Canadian customers
academic@hkeurope.com . . . . European customers
keycodesupport@hkaustralia.com . . . . Australian customers

HUMAN KINETICS
The Information Leader in Physical Activity

Product: Physical Education Technology Playbook, companion Web site

Key code: CASTELLI-J2J8H7AV-9780736060554

This unique code allows you access to the companion Web site